Slash Your
Retirement Risk

Slash Your Retirement Risk

How to Make Your Money Last With a Simple, Safe, and Secure Investment Plan

Chris Cook

CAREER
PRESS
Wayne, NJ

SLASH YOUR RETIREMENT RISK
Edited by Jodie Brandon
Typeset by Diana Ghazzawi
Cover design by Ty Nowicki
Chair Image by iDesign/shutterstock,
Palm tree image by Firuz Salamzadeh/shutterstock
Printed in the U.S.A.

To order this title, please call toll-free 1-800-CAREER-1 (NJ and Canada: 201 848 0310) to order using VISA or MasterCard, or for further information on books from Career Press.

The Career Press, Inc.
12 Parish Drive
Wayne, NJ 07470
www.careerpress.com

Library of Congress Cataloging-in-Publication Data

CIP Data Available Upon Request.

THIS BOOK IS DEDICATED to my amazing family. Thank you to my two wonderful children, Meaghan and Patrick, for making it clear to me that you would never take care of me in retirement. Thank you to my incredible wife, Katie, for reminding me the children are only partially kidding. The many hours of study and development that went into creating a better approach to retirement investing would have never been possible without your motivation. My retirement is secure because of you.

Contents

Introduction

THE PATH TO a healthy retirement nest egg has changed. Traditional buy-and-hold strategies that emphasize the return on your investments don't cut it anymore. Picking winners among blue-chip stocks or relying on high-interest bonds to generate enough money to last through retirement no longer carry the income guarantee they did in past generations.

Factor in today's global interdependent marketplace, our longer life spans, low interest rates, and extreme volatility in the markets, and without a shift in your approach to investing and saving, you very likely could run out of money in your lifetime.

Reliability of income—the "New ROI"—is what matters today. Retirement portfolios need to be managed using an investment strategy that's designed to make the most of your money's ability to grow while protecting it from what have become the all-too-frequent downsides.

The strategy should minimize risks and eliminate the emotion-driven investment decisions so common with the world's economic and political turmoil. And all this needs to happen while keeping costs and fees in check.

In our low-yield, rising-costs environment, investors simply can't afford not to invest in equities with their high-growth potential. The solution to slash your retirement risk, then, is to embrace a better strategy to equity investing—one designed to enhance growth and preserve gains. The New ROI does all that and more. It's a simple approach to stock investing and retirement saving that you can do yourself or with the guidance of a financial professional that can have a long-range positive effect on your financial future, as well as your personal peace of mind.

Typical retirement investment approaches can be too risky because they concentrate only on return on investments to build financial gains, and balance that with conservative "safe havens" such as bonds, CDs, Treasuries, and annuities. That's an outdated approach to generate gains and protect against losses, and fails to consider our low interest-rate environment and the dramatic ups and downs of today's markets.

From 2000 to 2015, the daily Standard & Poor's 500 (S&P 500) lost more than 2 percent of its value a total of 192 times. That compares with the previous 50 years in which the index lost 2 percent or more of its value only 160 times. Volatility *is* the new normal.

Investors today must do what's necessary to protect their retirement portfolios from what can be devastating losses associated with these more frequent equity downturns. If not, relying on typical investing approaches easily can result in financial disaster in the future.

To truly build a solid nest egg, investors need to recognize today's market realities and learn to embrace a strategy that focuses on creating an income stream in retirement that's reliable, is consistent, and can last a lifetime. The goal should be to set up an investment portfolio that can accomplish growth *and* income reliability over the long term. That's the New ROI equity investing strategy.

Looking to equities to generate a reliable income stream in retirement isn't a new concept. Most equities-based strategies, though, generally promise security based on what are inadequate asset allocations or diversifications, and may not be enough today to generate the income required to help guarantee long-term financial security in retirement.

Everyone, including people in or near retirement, must be prepared for today's wild market swings and potentially big losses that can accompany them. With the right moves now, your investments and money can survive the devastating downs and continue to thrive and provide the cash needed to live on later.

Today's right retirement strategy—the New ROI—means optimizing risk and maximizing gains, even amid the constant turmoil of the global economic picture.

Your retirement portfolio must have the ability to capitalize on market upsides and, at minimum, be able to generate enough income to keep up with inflation. As unbelievable as it may sound, many traditional strategies today barely keep up. With interest rates still relatively low, the earnings on a 10-year Treasury struggle to keep pace with the average historical rate of inflation—about 3 percent. Plus, it takes much more than simply breaking even to grow a nest egg to meet your retirement needs.

Even if someone stuffs wads of cash under the mattress, unless that mattress is magical and can grow that cash by more than the average rate of inflation each year, future financial security can be a losing battle.

Slash Your Retirement Risk shows investors how to develop a sound investment plan that will take them comfortably through retirement. Although plenty of people talk about various elements of the New ROI equity-investing strategy, too often implementation comes up short. In these pages, you'll find out why many other retirement investing approaches miss the mark and what it takes to make the New ROI work for you. Backed by mathematics and research from Nobel Prize–winning economists, investors, and experts, this scientific approach to equities investing can help provide your portfolio the results you need and want.

In these pages, you'll learn what to do and why, and how to create your own portfolio with the New ROI approach, either on your own or with the help of the right advisor. You'll understand why traditional approaches aren't enough.

I understand what can happen using the wrong approach to investing for retirement. As founder of Ohio-based Beacon Capital Management and a seasoned financial expert, I saw first-hand the financial devastation that so many people suffered after the Internet bubble burst in 2000. That's when I decided successful investing for today and tomorrow had to include not only the potential for gains, but also a focus on what could happen with the downsides. Thus, the Beacon Capital Management equity investing strategy—the foundation for the New ROI—was born.

That Beacon strategy has evolved today into a national network of investment advisors and advice that calls for sophisticated processes and ongoing monitoring systems—all based on my unique investment philosophy that focuses on investment management solutions that are calculated and risk management strategies that are pre-emptive and mechanical. The goal is to maximize the equity portion of a portfolio to capitalize on market upsides, while protecting against dramatic losses on the downside.

Now a simplified version of that strategy—the New ROI—is available to you. In these pages, you'll learn how to significantly cut back the risk to the equities in your portfolio and at the same time increase the opportunities your money has to grow and thrive. Whether you opt for a do-it-yourself approach or turn to the right financial advisor, the New ROI can help better ensure a reliable stream of income in retirement.

This is not the typical retirement portfolio approach based on doom and gloom predictions, preparing for the worst and hoping the money doesn't run out, promoting exotic investments, fleeing to gold bars, or touting expensive planning. Instead, this is a next-generation successful retirement portfolio strategy that utilizes technology and years of scientific economic analysis. The New ROI removes the emotion associated with much of today's investment decisions, relying instead on mechanical models that employ stop-loss strategies.

Slash Your Retirement Risk will show you how to realistically approach retirement investing in today's roller-coaster market environment. You'll understand how to look at what's happening in the markets today, as well as what to look at in terms of past performance, so you can end up with a portfolio capable of providing reliable income over the long term. You'll walk away comfortable in knowing how to invest to better ensure a lasting positive outcome for you and your loved ones.

So, if you're ready to transform your financial future, let's get started on the journey.

Part

1 Why Traditional Investment Strategies No Longer Work

1 The Failures of Traditional Investment Strategies

RELIABILITY OF INCOME—the "New ROI"—is not a get-rich-quick scheme or about unrealistic returns amid historically volatile times. If you're looking for a hot stock tip or the latest market trend, then you'll have to look elsewhere, too. However, if you want a simple approach to equity investing and retirement saving based on sound fundamentals and Nobel Prize–winning scientific analysis, then you have come to the right place.

Because we live in volatile times—defined by market extremes and great economic and militaristic upheavals—our investment decisions can end up marked by greed or fear. Investors often look for home-run returns or it seems like they're stuffing their money under the mattress. Neither of those approaches will help achieve your retirement goals.

Unlike other investment strategies, the New ROI recognizes that the best strategy is one that embraces equities for their high-growth potential and partners that with portfolio diversification and stop-loss models to hedge against catastrophic losses that have become all too frequent in today's marketplace.

In these pages, I'll give you the tools and the information to implement the New ROI on your own or with the help of a financial professional. With either approach, you'll learn what it takes to build a portfolio that can generate the income to keep you comfortable through your retirement.

To better understand the New ROI and why it's vital to grow and protect assets into and throughout your retirement, we first need to better understand traditional investment strategies—why they were the right choice for generations of Americans, but why they no longer are enough today.

Outdated Strategies

Post–World War II, the typical approach to retirement security focused on aggressive growth in the wealth accumulation phase followed by a very healthy distribution phase in which retirees could earn as much as 14 percent on safe-haven products such as bonds, CDs, Treasuries, and annuities.

It was a simple formula that worked. People poured their savings into equities like blue-chip stocks because, with a baby boom, real estate boom, and burgeoning infrastructure, everything tied to the U.S. economy seemed on an upward trajectory. There still were bear markets (1966 to 1978, for example), but strong returns from safe investment products still allowed retirees an option to continue to grow their assets while on a fixed income.

Those times have changed. With today's low interest rates, safe-haven investment options often don't even keep up with the rate of inflation. Investors actually can lose real equity while parking their assets in investments like CDs. Even though the Federal Reserve has begun to increase the federal funds rate after a half-dozen years of near-zero rates, those investments remain an unlikely ally to help an investor build the kind of cushion he or she will need in retirement.

Fig 1.1 Yields For Traditional Portfolios Have Fallen Below 4%

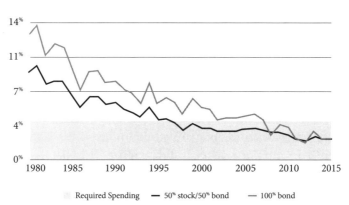

Required Spending   — 50% stock/50% bond   — 100% bond

Note: Based on the dividend yield of the Standard & Poor's 500 Index and the interest rate of the 10-year U.S. Treasury Bond.
Source: Standard and Poor's and Federal Reserve Board.

Today's investing environment—in which market volatility is the new norm—is an even bigger problem. Unfortunately, the traditional retirement investing strategies fail to take rapid market swings and the increasing frequency of bear markets into account, and no longer can deliver on their promises of growth along with protection for your nest egg.

Fig 1.2 Number of Days the S&P Declined by More Than 2%

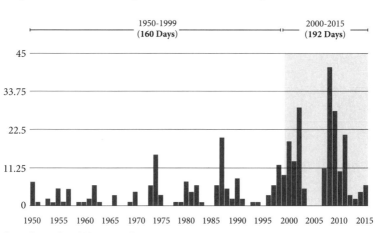

Source: Beacon Capital Management, Inc.

Tragic Realities

The new market realities have dashed the retirement dreams of millions of Americans.

Consider the case of Lou, a typical example of what's happened to so many retirees and their savings. Lou worked for years as an independent contractor. It was grueling work—mostly outdoors—but Lou did it, diligently saving and looking forward to finally slowing down at age 60 and relaxing in retirement. His last day at work was December 31, 1999. Lou had done his homework and determined that if he built a $500,000 nest egg and invested it in a balanced portfolio—split evenly between stocks and bonds—he could generate an income of $32,500 (6.5 percent) annually. It sounded good; Lou had the research to prove it, so he bought into the retirement investing approach.

The big problem, though, was the system didn't work. The new volatile market reality had begun. The bear market in 2000 and then another in 2008 took their toll on Lou's nest egg and his future financial security. Fifteen years after he retired, Lou's retirement savings were decimated. As of December 31, 2015, at age 75 he was left with just $73,000. The years of hard work had taken their toll on Lou's health, too, to the point where he faced hefty annual medical-related, out-of-pocket expenses. His is a scary financial future no one wants to have to face.

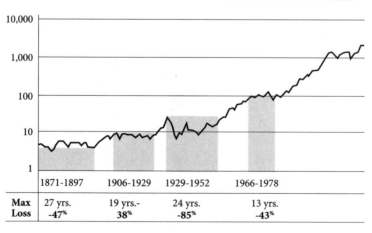

Fig. 1.3 History of S&P 500 Bear Markets

Bear Markets	
Average Duration	19 yrs.
Average Max Loss	-53%

	1871-1897	1906-1929	1929-1952	1966-1978
Max Loss	27 yrs. -47%	19 yrs.- 38%	24 yrs. -85%	13 yrs. -43%

Note: S&P 500 monthly data (1871-2015).

Are you willing to end up like Lou? From a retirement planning standpoint, Lou thought he had done everything right and that he and his wife would be financially set for life. He followed the popular approach that so many retirement planning experts touted; his investment moves made sense on paper. The strategy he followed had worked for his own father and for millions more Americans for decades. But Lou came up short because the traditional investment strategies no longer work.

Real Risks and Fallacies

Throughout the 20th century, we saw various iterations of this traditional portfolio strategy. Investors looked to create security by mixing equities for financial gains with conservative "safe havens" such as bonds, CDs, and Treasuries. The portfolio might be split 50-percent stocks to generate growth and 50-percent bonds for security.

Any chart that shows the projected income of this portfolio over the long term often paints a picture of future income curves that arc smoothly upward in the first years and early into retirement, and then, as withdrawals continue, slowly tapers off.

Fig. 1.4 Constant Return

8.7% Constant Return

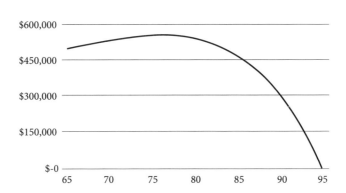

Note: Annual withdrawal starting at age 65 is 6.5% (32,500) increased each year by 3.1%.

Figure 1.4 depicts a $500,000 retirement portfolio with a very realistic long-term 8.7-percent return (that's the historical average since 1927 for a portfolio split between 50-percent stocks and 50-percent bonds), and calls for regular 6.5 percent annual withdrawals—$32,500 a year—which increases each year to account for inflation and not run out of money for 30 years.

Unfortunately, that portfolio mix and the income arc in Figure 1.4 can be misleading because both count on an *average* projected return for the portfolio, and not the dramatic ups and downs of the stock market that are rapidly becoming more commonplace in today's markets.

Looking at the markets over time—in this case, 1927–2015—that portfolio may *average* an 8.7-percent return. But that time period includes roller-coaster market years, including a worst one-year performance: a 22.8-percent loss in 1931. Losses in 2008 came close to the 1931 record, but didn't surpass it.

You can begin to see the problem and the trap for people who have saved and invested like Lou. What if it was 2008, and you had planned to retire soon or even the same year that markets dropped 20-plus percent? The chances are good that your portfolio might not recover enough in time—if ever—to meet your projected financial needs in retirement.

The greater the volatility of the market, the more hits on a nest egg that follows traditional retirement investing strategies—and the less reliable any projected income in retirement.

Why the Big Failure?

There's no single reason why traditional investment strategies no longer work. A complex set of factors—from market volatility to global economic interdependence, geopolitical turmoil, and more—all play a role in wreaking havoc on retirement investing plans.

Let's look more closely at these factors to better understand why old strategies come up short in the new market reality.

Market Volatility

Theories abound regarding the causes of the increased market volatility—from the threat of terrorism and violence, to globalization and interdependence of businesses and industries, the prevalence of protracted economies, civil and political unrest, increased computerized program trading, and the simple fact that more people are trading in the markets today.

Almost anyone with an Internet connection can become a stock trader. That can be problematic for markets, because individuals tend to make investment decisions based on emotions such as fear or greed. In turn, what ends up as mass emotional buys and sells can reinforce dramatic price and market swings.

Less-experienced traders also tend to react more often to what are typical minor shifts in an industry or a sector. A drop of a few percentage points in several stocks in one industry, for example, could prompt a sell-off. Or some great new idea might prompt a buy, no matter the stock price, company earnings—or lack thereof—or other fundamentals.

Longevity

Compounding the saving-for-retirement challenge, people are living longer today, which means their money has to last longer, too. The average American male who turned 65 in 2016 can expect to live 18 more years, while the average woman survives another 20.6 years, according to data from the National Center for Health Statistics.[1]

Adding to those numbers, the latest actuary tables show there's a one-in-four chance you or your spouse/significant other will live well into your 90s.

As the safety net for financial security in retirement, Social Security, which was signed into law in 1935 by President Franklin Roosevelt, never was meant to take care of Americans' needs for a retirement lasting decades. In fact, in 1930 the average life expectancy for men was just 58 and for women, 62.[2]

Times and longevity definitely have changed. Without planning ahead for the potential for longevity and today's market volatility, you very well could outlive your money. That's the number-one retirement fear facing nearly six in 10 Americans, according to a 2015 survey from the American Institute of CPAs.[3]

Fig. 1.5 Top Retirement Concerns

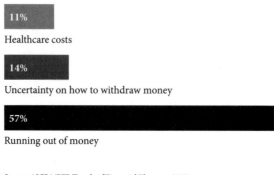

Source: AICPA/PFP Trends of Financial Planners, 2015.

Rising Healthcare Costs

Americans clearly worry—and for good reasons—about the wildly spiraling upward cost of healthcare, too, and its effects on saving for and living through retirement. In the year 2000, Americans spent an average $4,857 per capita on healthcare, according to Centers for Disease Control numbers. By 2014, that per capita average nearly doubled to $9,523, and the numbers are projected to only go higher through the end of the decade. And these are in terms out-of-pocket costs, not the cost of insurance.

Of even more concern, a 65-year-old couple in 2015 would need to have $392,000 in targeted savings to give them a 90-percent chance of having saved enough by age 65 to pay for their healthcare expenses in retirement. That's up $65,000 from 2014's $326,000, according to the latest statistics from the nonprofit Employee Benefit Research Institute. And those numbers don't include any savings to cover the cost of long-term care if necessary. That can add tens of thousands of dollars per year to those expenses.[4]

The bottom line means more pressure on a retirement portfolio to produce enough growth and still remain protected from potential dramatic and possibly devastating losses.

The New Retirement Lifestyle

As if all the above factors weren't enough to rethink how to invest and save for retirement, there's more. The Baby Boomer generation has redefined the meaning of retirement. Likely when your grandparents retired, the need for cash declined, too, because retirement back then usually meant quietly living out your few remaining years without having to work. For financial planning purposes, 70 percent of pre-retirement income was considered enough to fund the rest of your life.

Not anymore. Today's retirees are more active than ever before, engaged in every imaginable pastime. Whether it's volunteering halfway around the world, or traveling the world, a new second or third career, entrepreneurship, artistic endeavors, or simply enjoying the great (and costly) things that life has to offer, it takes a lot of money today to be "retired."

Poor Diversification Strategy

The traditional investment strategy offered a diversity of investments such as stocks, bonds, mutual funds, real estate holdings, or commodities. The growth of markets and the lack of rapid downturns meant that investors like Lou could invest their money, earn great growth potential, and their portfolios have just enough protection to hedge against the limited volatility of the day. But as you've seen, the new market reality is a very different animal.

Lou's approach can be mortally flawed today because our global, interwoven marketplace and economies blur the traditional lines of diversification among industries, companies, countries, and sectors of the economy. What once were diverse and separate holdings now have become closely intertwined. Global interdependence could result from a company's or industry's reliance on global sales, international sources of raw material or services, offshore outsourcing, or something else. Whatever the reason, though, that interdependence can seriously skew the models investors and their advisors use to supposedly help add diversity—and therefore protection—to their retirement investment portfolios.

Fig 1.6 Estimated Percent of S&P 500 Company Sales

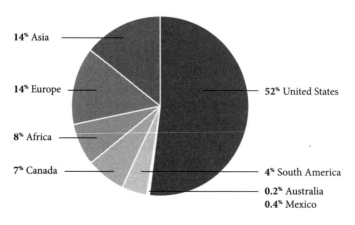

14% Asia

14% Europe

8% Africa

7% Canada

52% United States

4% South America

0.2% Australia
0.4% Mexico

Source: http://www.marketwatch.com/story/sp-500-companies-generate-barely-over-half-their-revenue-at-home-2015-08-19. Data: S&P Dow Jones Indices. Calculations: Steve Goldstein.

More than 47 percent of the sales of the S&P 500 companies are derived in countries outside of the United States. It makes complete sense that traditional diversification strategies, such as U.S. and international holdings, are not as effective with almost half the revenues of our largest companies generated internationally.[5]

The Inflation Effect

Denise decided the best approach to retirement savings was to diligently put a little money away every month. Then, when she had enough cash stashed, she would buy certificates of deposit and Treasuries. She figured it was a great way to save, build wealth, and ensure the safety of her money. She also figured the money eventually would grow into a huge nest egg to pass to her nieces and nephews (she didn't have any children).

Denise modeled her savings plan after that of a favorite aunt who had done the same thing and ended up very comfortable. Even after paying hefty, out-of-pocket, long-term-care expenses for several years, her aunt died with an estate worth well more than $1 million.

The flaw in the plan, though—as Denise is beginning to see after only five years—is that her aunt was investing her money in CDs and Treasuries at a time when double-digit returns were possible—not the very low interest rate environment of today that barely, if at all, keeps up with inflation.

Denise found out the hard way that except in specific market conditions or circumstances—like a sudden drastic market downturn—investors simply can't afford to leave major portions of their assets in fixed income investments like CDs, annuities, and bonds.

Fig. 1.7 1-Year CD Rates

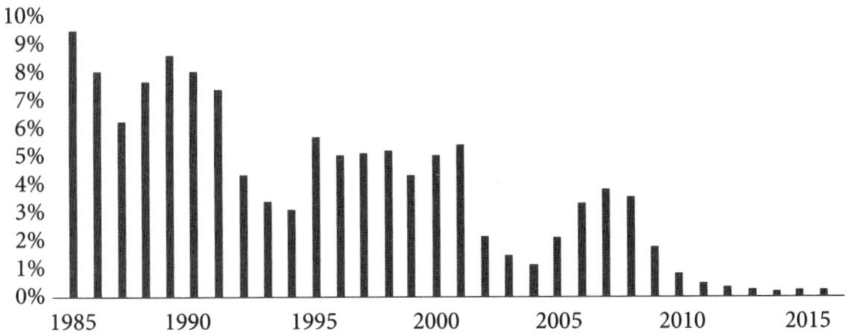

Note: Figures do not add to 100% due to multiple responses. Source: Siegal & Gale LLC, "Investor Research Report" for the SEC, July 26, 2012, p. 72; *www.sec.gov/news/studies/2012/917-financial-literacy-study-part3.pdf.*

As Denise's situation reflects, the cost of inflation is too often overlooked by investors seeking safe haven amid volatile times. In the new market reality, even the one-time "safe bets" aren't, and can have a devastating effect on retirement plans.

Fig. 1.8 Cost of Inflation

Item	1972	1995	2010*
Postage Stamp	8¢	32¢	54¢
Carton of Milk	30¢	$1.43	$2.43
New Car	$3,879	$18,360	$31, 135

*Source: BLS.gov.

James Poterba, the president of the National Bureau of Economic Research (NBER) and a researcher at the Massachusetts Institute of Technology, examined the dollars-and-cents toll that low interest rates exact on investing and saving to fund your retirement. What he found should be enough to shock all of us into taking a new and better approach to retirement investing:

> In 1993, when the average yield on AAA corporate bonds was 7.9 percent, the annual payout per dollar of annuity premium for a single-premium immediate annuity purchased by a 65-year-old male was 9.7 percent. Twelve years later, in 2005, when the AAA rate was 5.4 percent, the annuity payout was 7.8 percent. In 2013, when the AAA rate averaged 3.8 percent, the annuity payout was 6.3 percent. An individual who had been accumulating resources with the goal of financing a specific retirement income target would have needed 24 percent more wealth in 2013 than in 2005 to meet this goal.[6]

That study was completed a few years ago. Current AAA corporate bond rates, according to internal Beacon Capital Management, Inc. calculations, are hovering even lower—less than 3.5 percent today, leaving an estimated payout from a single-premium immediate annuity at 6.0 percent or less. However, that 6-percent number can be a bit misleading because with an immediate annuity, the holder is locked into the contract, and it's tough to escape. If you do, you—or your heirs—must surrender the principle. If, for example, you die before the annuity is paid out, the insurance company issuing the annuity keeps what's left.

The bottom line: As we saw with Denise and from the NBER study, parking your money in any one of those traditionally considered safe vehicles, except for emergencies or to provide quick access to cash, is a losing proposition. That strategy worked for previous generations, but not in today's new market reality.

Actively Managed No Guarantee

Relying wholly on a financial professional to time markets, buy and sell to generate gains, and know when and how to avoid losses, may not be enough to protect and grow a nest egg either.

Too many experts cling to the traditional investment strategies, and in doing so, may realize big gains, but too often leave themselves and their clients vulnerable to the big downturns that can ruin retirement plans.

Later in the book, I'll talk more about how to find the right financial advisor, whether you need one, or if you should consider doing it yourself. Either approach can work if you embrace the New ROI.

Over the next several chapters, we will examine the New ROI, why it works, how you can make it work, and why you should take advantage of it now.

Last Words

Let's review some of the essentials discussed in this chapter:

- Today's retirement looks very different from that of several decades ago. People are living longer, costs for everything are increasing, and lifestyles have changed.

- Forget sitting around in a rocking chair; retirement has become an active, exciting, and more expensive time in many people's lives.

- That means more pressure on retirement savings to provide a reliable and ample income stream in retirement.

- Volatility is the new normal when it comes to investing today.

- Our low interest-rate environment further undermines traditional approaches to retirement investing.

- The rate of inflation cannot be ignored when building an investment plan.

- Retirees can no longer depend on safe-haven investments to help grow their nest eggs.

- Rising healthcare costs will take up an increasing percentage of Americans' retirement savings.

- Traditional investment strategies that worked for generations of Americans are now an outdated and unsuccessful approach to hitting your retirement goals.

Now It's Your Turn

To help you take control of your investing portfolio with the New ROI in mind, some questions to ask yourself about your investing, portfolio, and financial future include:

- In our uncertain economic times, do you worry about your financial future? If so, you're not alone. Six in 10 American workers are concerned they'll run out of money in their lifetimes.

- Have you thought about the importance of reliability of an income stream in retirement? It matters, especially in our uncertain economic times.

- What have you done, if anything, to help ensure a reliable financial future? Your portfolio should be allocated so that your investments have the opportunity to grow enough to provide the income you'll need in retirement.

- Is your portfolio allocated to capitalize on market upswings? In today's volatile investing environment, equities are a vital part of the mix.

- Or, are you betting your future financial security on traditional safe havens such as bonds, Treasuries, and CDs? Many of these traditionally conservative and safe investments barely—if at all—earn enough income to keep up with the average rate of inflation—generally about 3 percent annually.

- Is your retirement nest egg parked in money market funds or savings accounts? Except for your emergency stash, these traditional savings vehicles are a losing proposition if you want to reach your retirement goals.

- Does your retirement investing strategy count on expensive advice, look to exotic investments, or count gold bars in its mix? These are not reliable approaches to provide your money the opportunities and protection it needs to grow.

- Does your portfolio include capital protection from today's all-too-frequent market downturns? It should, but holding your money as cash for long periods of time isn't the answer, either. Again, it's about inflation and how it erodes a portfolio that doesn't have adequate growth opportunities.

2 In Pursuit of Reliable Income: The "New ROI"

NOW THAT YOU understand why traditional investment strategies can fall short when it comes to your retirement goals, it's time to take a new approach: the "New ROI."

Today's investor needs an investment strategy that captures aggressive equity growth while accounting for extreme market volatility, economic uncertainty, and geopolitical upheaval, which have become all too common in recent times. Investors also need triggers in place to protect them against bear markets that can wreck retirement dreams.

The New ROI approach to equity investing recognizes all of today's investing realities and is designed to give your money the opportunity to capitalize on market upsides while minimizing losses on the downside.

A New Twist on Value-Added Total Returns

Typically, investors think about growing an equity investment in terms of whether the price of that investment goes up or down and whether it might provide any fixed income in the future. That can be misleading, though, because to accurately lay out a retirement investment strategy you must take into consideration an investment's total return—including factors like interest, dividends, distributions, capital gains, taxes, and fees.

Total return investing takes all that into consideration plus includes portfolio rebalancing to ensure the portfolio maintains its diversification, and looks to low-cost, tax-efficient investments like ETFs (exchange-traded funds) to keep fees manageable.

With the New ROI strategy, your portfolio has the broadest possible diversification and built-in protections against precipitous and costly market drops.

This is a method of retirement investing—or any investing plan—that can be maintained throughout your lifetime. Plus, it can better ensure that a retirement portfolio will not only last through the necessary potential decades required, but also provide consistent returns no matter the external economic situation of the moment.

This is value-added total return investing with an additional twist, and it's a retirement planning necessity in today's low-yield, rising-costs environment.

Let's look more closely at what makes the New ROI work in today's marketplace.

Essential Elements of the New ROI

The New ROI approach to equities investing for retirement includes:

- **Understanding clearly the New ROI mindset, and how it makes a difference.** With today's roller-coaster markets—and subsequent crippling losses that can occur—an individual's investment approach—for retirement or anything else—must work to help ensure he or she will have a *reliable* future income. That means, despite external economics and up and down markets, you can expect and count on receiving a steady income throughout your retirement years. Without this kind of built-in protection, an equity portfolio and your financial future can be vulnerable.

- **Maintaining investing discipline by utilizing effective risk management to eliminate emotional investment decisions.** Getting the emotion out of investing decisions is essential, especially in today's chaotic economic and political environment. That means establishing and sticking to specific and scientifically derived parameters related to what and when to buy and sell, how to balance a portfolio's allocations, and how often to rebalance those allocations. Though some mutual funds have created clever target-date retirement funds that can provide 24/7 rebalancing and attentiveness thanks to automatic systems, there is another way. It's an approach that offers real portfolio diversification and often ends up less expensive because you're not paying a variety of fees for services. Individual investors can direct their own emotion-free investing with this New ROI system.

- **Maximizing diversification: Risk mitigation begins with real and strong diversification.** Too often, what investors think is a diversified stock portfolio really isn't. For example, many mutual funds invest in the same companies. Although you may think you're diversifying by investing in different funds, the reality is that you may not be. To help avoid unnecessary overexposure or underexposure to any one sector of the economy, the New ROI spreads risk broadly and equally across 11 investment sectors: healthcare, consumer staples, consumer discretionary, real estate, technology, financials, energy, industrials, telecommunications, materials, and utilities.

- **Minimizing losses: Effective risk management curbs investment losses before they become destructive.** The New ROI lays out parameters for and helps you build in simple stop-loss protections for portfolios. When the S&P 500 drops a predetermined amount—our research has shown that a drop of 10 percent is optimal—that's the trigger to "stop-loss" by selling your equities to limit your losses. The cash related to that sale then should be transferred temporarily into safer investments like more stable bond funds, U.S. Treasuries, or even held in a money market account until markets recover. With the do-it-yourself New ROI approach, the point of recovery and return to the market is simple, too: a rise of 15 percent in the S&P 500 benchmark index.

- **Keeping management fees/costs at a minimum.** Plenty of people talk about low-cost investing. But implementation often comes up short because of costs associated with an investment management style (passive or active), excessive investment turnover, fees that can be hidden, overlooked, or unknown to an investor, and more. Even no-load mutual funds come with fees. The New ROI approach takes keeping fees low to a new level by capitalizing on low-cost investing options while also reminding investors to know and understand ahead of time all the fees associated with any investment, what those fees buy and what they don't, and why, and then factoring all that into a portfolio's overarching investment goals.

New Approach, Solid Science

As you can see, this New ROI approach isn't about buy low/sell high, timing markets, or making every penny possible on every investment and every market upside. It's about protecting a nest egg from what can be devastating losses that can happen when markets drop, while also providing a portfolio the opportunity to capitalize on market gains on the upside.

The New ROI is backed by scientific analysis of markets and research from Nobel Prize–winning economists, investors, and experts. (I'll talk more about the details in later chapters.) And, in case you were wondering, the New ROI has a solid track record with numbers to back it up, too.

Fig 2.1 Historical Performance

	New ROI	S&P 500
YTD	10.02%	7.58%
1 Year	7.52%	5.46%
3 Years	10.15%	10.99%
5 Years	10.00%	13.20%
10 Years	9.20%	7.62%
20 Years	10.40%	8.21%

Data: Back-tested simulation ending July 31, 2016.
S&P 500 data provided by Standard & Poor's.

Losses Have Greater Impacts Than Gains

Bear markets or even brief dramatic downturns can devastate a portfolio with lasting consequences. For example, a 35-percent loss takes much more than a 35-percent gain to break even. Compounding the initial loss, what's left of the investment has to work that much harder and longer to recover. A 35-percent loss needs a 54-percent gain just to return to even.

If someone is already retired and counting on that portfolio for living expenses and making regular withdrawals, a portfolio's recovery efforts are further stressed as those withdrawals add to the losses and take away from the gains.

I'll get into more detail about the power of losses later. But for now, let's look briefly at what happened to the average investor's portfolio in the most recent bear market in 2008. When that devastating year finally ended, the S&P 500 had lost 37 percent of its value. At the same time, a portfolio that followed the strategies outlined in this book ended the year in positive territory!

Not an Unusual Case

In case you think 2008 was an exception and likely won't happen again, markets have dropped 10 percent or more a total of 29 times since 1926. During the 2007–2008 bear, investors lost more than $10 trillion, according to U.S. Government Accountability Office estimates, because diversification alone wasn't enough.[1]

Although the average sector fared better than traditional asset classes, the losses were still too much for most investors. Even the best-balanced portfolios lost more than 20 percent.

Fig. 2.2 2008 Asset Class Returns

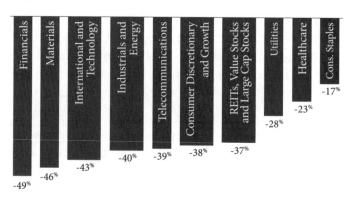

Source: Beacon Capital Management, Inc. (Sector Returns)
and Dimensional Fund Advisors (Asset Class Returns).

Smaller Spread

Over 10 years as of July 31, 2015, an equity portfolio based on the New ROI strategy would have had an annualized return of 9.20 percent, compared with the S&P 500's 7.62 percent.

Since 1994 (the onset of the New ROI's scientific tracking), the returns are 10.40 percent for the New ROI and 8.21 percent for the S&P.

Peace of Mind

The returns are similar in these previous two scenarios, so why bother making a change to the New ROI? Keep in mind what can happen to a portfolio—and your nest egg—in a bear market like that of 2008.

Retirement investing should be about peace of mind, removing the day-to-day and month-to-month worry about your financial future. Today's volatile markets include regular downsides that can seriously impact portfolios. Remember earlier what happened to Lou and his nest egg? Your nest egg should be protected from the downturns and still be able to grow to meet your future needs.

In Figure 2.3, the light-gray line represents the performance over time of a portfolio based on the New ROI approach compared with that of a traditional portfolio without built-in stop-loss protections. The performance includes annual withdrawals starting at $32,500 and increasing every year.

As you can see, minimizing losses has a dramatic effect on returns and, more importantly, income.

Fig. 2.3 Historical Performance With Withdrawals

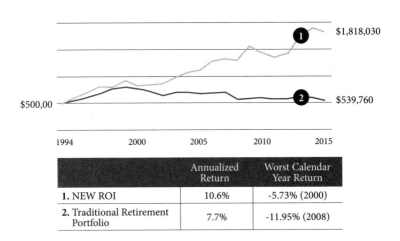

	Annualized Return	Worst Calendar Year Return
1. NEW ROI	10.6%	-5.73% (2000)
2. Traditional Retirement Portfolio	7.7%	-11.95% (2008)

Notes: Annual withdrawal is 6.5% ($32,500) increased each year by 3.1%.
Annual Rebalancing. Traditional Retirement Portfolio is allocated and represented with 50% S&P 500 and 50% Barclays Aggregate Bond.
Data: Back-tested simulation January 1, 1994 – December 31, 2015. S&P 500 data provided by Standard & Poor's. Barclays Aggregate Bond data provided by CRSP.

Getting Started

With the New ROI equity approach to building a retirement nest egg, you don't have to count on the mixed prowess of decision-making by others. You won't have to deal with fallout from buy/sell moves made in the emotion of the moment or worry about the economic and political turmoil of the day and its effects and how they may or may not affect your equity investments and financial future.

With the New ROI approach to investing, you can better ensure you'll have the cash in hand that you need throughout your retirement.

In the following pages, you'll learn more about this next-generation approach to retirement investing. I'll explain step by step how to build and maintain a New ROI equity portfolio as part of your total retirement portfolio—either on your own, or to maximize the advantages and the returns, with the help of the right financial advisor.

Last Words

Let's review some of the essentials discussed in this chapter:

- The new ROI approach to equity investing is designed to capture market upsides while keeping protections against devastating bear markets that can wipe out retirement plans.

- Today's investors must focus on *reliable* future income to reach their retirement goals. That means expecting and counting on steady income throughout their retirement years.

- Removing emotion from investment decisions and relying instead on mechanical models helps investors realize their financial dreams.

- A successful approach to retirement saving today should include equities because of their potential for growth.

- The equity side of your portfolio also demands a diversification strategy that helps grow the portfolio while building in protections from the new volatile normal.

- Keep in mind that typically equity investments promise performance that counts on "average" projected returns, not today's reality, which is ongoing dramatic ups and downs in our rollercoaster markets.

- Downturns represent a real and lasting threat to your money and your financial future.

- Losses are much more powerful than gains because after a loss, it takes what's left of your money much longer to return to breakeven without even taking into consideration financial gains necessary to meet your future retirement needs.

- This New ROI approach isn't about buy low/sell high, timing markets, or making every penny possible on every investment and every market upside. Instead it's about capitalizing on market upsides while at the same time providing portfolio protection on the downsides.

- Today's right retirement strategy—the New ROI—means optimizing risk, maximizing gains, and taking into account the constant changes in the global economic picture.

Now It's Your Turn

To help you take control of your investing portfolio with the New ROI in mind, some questions to ask yourself about your investing, portfolio, and financial future include:

- Does your equity investment strategy embrace the tenets of the New ROI? If not, then you're not reaching your potential in the new market reality.

- Have you eliminated emotional investment decisions in your retirement plans? A mechanical model will help remove the human-related errors that can ruin nest eggs.

- Have you leaned too heavily on traditional safe haven investments like CDs? In the current rate environment, an over-reliance on these financial instruments will not help you reach your retirement goals.

- If you are in an aggressive growth phase, do you have enough of your assets invested in equities? Equities allow you the best growth potential.

- Do you have stop-loss protections in place to hedge against bear markets? In your investment life, the losses will impact your savings much more than the gains.

- Do you have peace of mind when you have equity investments in place? The New ROI is based on sound fundamentals and science-backed theories so you don't have to sweat each turn of the market.

3 Fallacies, Fantasies, and Biases in Today's Investment World

INVESTING SUCCESS in these times that call for the "New ROI" approach means positioning portfolios for success no matter the ups and downs of economies and markets, and the emotional responses to them.

It sounds simple, but it's not. We don't live (and invest) in a vacuum. Sales pitches of all kinds bombard us daily. People also develop personal biases related to investment decisions—and sometimes those decisions can wreck retirement plans.

Let's look more closely at some of the most common biases, fallacies, and fantasies in investing, and expose them for what they are: a hindrance to achieving your investing and retirement goals.

First Things First

Forget those hot investment tips of the moment and ignore the noise from friends, family, and self-proclaimed gurus. Whether they tout getting in on the latest and greatest investment deal, seeking out alternative investments, fleeing to safe havens, buying into big real estate deals, chasing top managers, or some other money-making scheme, the odds of success are not in your favor that this is the silver bullet.

Successful investing, after all, is not about silver bullets or magic beans. This isn't about fairy tales. When I talk with clients, we discuss their nest eggs, assets, and retirement dreams. And, we talk about these topics in real terms, using real-life scenarios, data-tested science, and economics, not pie-in-the-sky fantasies.

Evolutionary Biases

For those of us who have ever been drawn to or taken in by sales pitches—that's all of us at one time or another—it's important to realize it's human nature to respond to these come-ons. Often how we react to an investment tip or suggestion relates to our in-born human biases. The major biases affecting investing are fear and greed. That's not a negative commentary; it's the truth based on the wiring in our brains.

Think about how you might react if someone offered you the deal-of-a-lifetime with the promise of riches. It feels good. You may even decide to go for it. But, by the time your human survival instinct kicks in and you get the signal to run, it's too late. You've already lost your money.

Dropping markets create a similar scenario. When you notice the bottom is falling out, it's often too late to stem your losses, unless—as is a tenet of the New ROI equity management approach—you've planned ahead and have in place aggressive counter-measures.

Further complicating things, sometimes you get mixed messages or red flags that can leave you scared or confused as to the right way to react.

Let's look more closely at the potential damage to your retirement portfolio that this behavioral phenomenon may cause.

Risk Aversion

In the world of finance, investors show risk aversion when exposed to uncertainty. They tend to try to limit the uncertainty.

In theory, that sounds like good advice. I'm a strong proponent of reducing one's risk. The New ROI, too, includes triggers to hedge against risk. However, the approach can be abused.

Sometimes information or even misinformation persists that keeps investors from making sound financial decisions. For example, consider the argument over interest rates. The hot tip over the last few years has been that investors should avoid anything interest-rate sensitive because rates are going up.

Really? The "experts" go on to caution investors to avoid bonds because of the impending bear market that will accompany rising interest rates. And they warn investors to stay away from utilities and real estate because rising rates adversely affect both. By the way, some warn, too, to avoid equities because they're just too volatile in our uncertain political and economic times.

The issue of concern to investors is that when rates rise, bond prices typically fall because bond prices move inversely to interest rates. Therefore, when rates rise, bonds are less advantageous to own, and vice versa.

Before anyone gives in and follows the advice of the doom-and-gloom prognosticators, though, let's not forget that these same experts have been predicting for the past five years that rates would go up. Rates didn't climb until late 2015, and then only slightly. These experts also have spent at least the last four years cautioning about the coming bear market in the bond world.

Accepting the New Normal

The reality is that volatility is the new norm. When the Fed raised interest rates in December 2015 for the first time since June 2006, bonds didn't tank. In fact, at the end of the third quarter 2016, bonds were up 5.80 percent for the year to date; utilities were up 15.8 percent, and real estate was up 7.9 percent. That compares with the S&P 500, which was up 7.7 percent.

Despite my personal concern about potential interest rate increases, Beacon Capital's client portfolios have continued to prosper as interest rates stagnated near historic lows.

Rather than allow emotional responses to markets into the investing equation, we offer advice to our clients based on scientifically derived parameters. Otherwise, over the last five years our clients might well have avoided bonds and utilities, and lost out on the considerable upward momentum of the markets. These investments—along with equities in general—have continued to climb.

Let's consider what could have happened to your money if you had allowed the fear of market volatility and the perception of impending rising interest rates to affect your investing decisions. Let's assume that you had opted to pull your money out of stocks and bonds and sat on the sidelines.

In dollars and cents, that risk aversion cost your portfolio dearly. Parking your portfolio in cash cost you not only in terms of inflation but in lost returns. Despite market uncertainties, in 2014 alone, the 10-year U.S. Treasury bond earned 10.75 percent. That meant if your portfolio was valued at $100,000, in that year alone you lost $10,750 in gains without factoring in inflation.

Cut Through the Noise

Another factor that can adversely affect your retirement investing is the constant noise. When you're bombarded with all the different sales pitches and "experts" who claim to know what's going on investing-wise, how do you learn to ignore it? Unfortunately, sometimes people don't.

Art and Marie, both well-educated and successful businesspeople, are clients with whom I've worked for a number of years. During a year-end review in 1999, Art came to me with a proposal to buy a significant amount of stock in Cisco Systems (NASDAQ: CSCO).

Apparently, a friend of the couple, someone they knew personally and professionally and trusted implicitly, had recommended the stock. Their friend, Nancy, who lived and worked in the San Francisco Bay Area, had been investing in Cisco and truly believed the company's annual double-digit returns were unstoppable. After all, Cisco was on the cutting edge of the technology and internet revolution.

To his credit, Art made a compelling pitch to buy the stock, complete with numbers and projections of nothing but big growth ahead. Fortunately, as you've seen in these pages, I'm not a fan of hot stocks or jumping on the latest bandwagon. I persuaded Art and Marie not to pin their entire financial future on Cisco. They agreed to invest only $25,000 in the company's stock. When the dot-com bubble burst two years later, that $25,000 became $10,000. Nearly 15 years after its stock collapse, Cisco's stock still hasn't returned to those 1999 levels.

The Bubble Craze

To avoid a similar hit to your portfolio, it's important to be able to recognize when an economic surge in a sector or stock has crossed over and become another bubble filling up with hot air. The best indicator is when an asset begins trading at levels that strongly deviate from its intrinsic value.

Buyer beware because bubbles aren't going away. They have become mainstays of economic cycles since their debut in the 1600s.

We read about bubbles; sometimes we experience them, and we think we learn from them. But then another bubble happens and investors—drawn to the bright light of a big return—see their finances ruined.

In the first half of 2015, we had another bubble—a mini-biotech craze. On July 17, 2015, the NASDAQ Biotech Index hit a new high: 4,162.82. Investors were counting their cash. Retirees and soon-to-be retirees banking on biotech were planning their world cruises and envisioning zero financial worries ahead.

The bubble kept growing despite the warning signs. In April that year, Wyatt Investment Research's Jay Taylor pointed to a looming threat. He noted that the three top performing stocks for 2015 as of that date were biotechs—Eagle Pharmaceuticals (NASDAQ: EGRX), Amarin Corporation (NASDAQ: Amarin), and Pfenex (NASDAQ: PFNX)—and none was currently profitable. At the time, Eagle was trading around $52 a share; Amarin traded in the vicinity of $1.90, and Pfenex was just above $13 a share.[1]

Fig. 3.1 The Biotech Bubble

Stock (Symbol)	Jan. 1, 2015 Price	Apr. 30, 2015 Price	Apr. 30, 2016 Price	Jan. 1, 2015- Apr. 30 2015 Performance	Apr. 30, 2015- Apr. 30, 2016 Performance
Eagle Pharmaceuticals (EGRX)	$15.50	$52.70	$37.86	240%	-28%
Amarin Corporation (AMRN)	$0.98	$1.92	$1.83	96%	-5%
Pfenex (PFNX)	$7.18	$13.35	$8.16	86%	-39%

By May, concerned about the underlying financials, Federal Reserve Chairman Janet Yellen also cautioned investors to beware of the overstretched valuations in biotech.[2]

But the warnings went unheeded, and biotech kept climbing—albeit a bit circuitously. Buyers kept buying, too. Then, like the technology bubble before it, the biotech bubble suddenly burst. By September 25, 2015, the index had dropped nearly 1,000 points to 3,246.11. In typical roller-coaster fashion, the index pulled out a small end-of-the-year rally before plunging again in early 2016, its days of glory appear over at least for the moment.

Fig. 3.2 NASDAQ Biotech Index

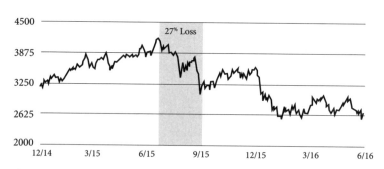

Source: www.finance.yahoo.com.

For those who bought into the bubble and banked on it, the losses were staggering and the lessons tough to learn. Unless investors cashed out at the top before the bubble collapsed, those dreams of world cruises and promises of financial security are off the table, for now.

Melina, a pharmacy technician, and her husband, Mark, a school teacher, believed in biotech's strength. Though they had both seen friends lose so much in the financial collapse of 2008, they still invested Melina's 401(k) heavily in the stock of the company where she worked, AVEO Pharmaceuticals. They didn't worry about diversifying, either, because they were sure their holdings were safe and secure and headed for the financial moon. After all, AVEO focused on promising treatments for cancer. It was a win-win. Melina and Mark figured they could make money on their investment, and those investments could be used to help in the battle against a dreaded disease.

Then came the biotech bust. AVEO's stock price, which topped $1.29 a share in January 2016, had fallen to less than 70 cents as of October 2016. In only 10 months, the couple lost 46 percent of their portfolio.

People often seem to insist that things will be different the next time around and that they know what they are doing. Things usually aren't that different, as Melina and Mark found out, and it's almost always too late before we wake up to reality. It's a real lesson that too few investors recognize until after they've suffered the consequences.

More Investment Fantasies That Fall Flat

Other investing blind spots lurk out there, too. Some may seem manageable, others harmless, and still others tried-and-true investment strategies. Harmless or not, all of them can stand in the way of your achieving your financial goals.

Let's look at a few.

Market Timing

Timing the markets can be another of those losing investment propositions. Thousands of organizations and their investment specialists tout proprietary formulas, tips, and tricks to master the never-ending and often-erratic ups and downs of everyday bulls and bears. Each usually claims to have a sure-fire secret to when to make an initial equities buy—at the lowest price point, of course—or the right time to sell—at the price pinnacle.

Corporations constantly struggle to time their equities buybacks, too. In reality, though, companies and their in-house experts rarely time the buybacks of their own stocks to coincide with the stock's lowest price.

No matter who is trying—S&P 500 companies or individual investors—few actually succeed at market-timing. If the experts can't do it, the chances of success for an individual investor are likely even less.

In fact, many buybacks happen at exactly the wrong time. A company may think it's doing great or that it has come up with the greatest new product or service and decides now is the time to buy back stock. But then the product or service fizzles and so does the company. Think about the debut of the Samsung Galaxy Note 7, the cell phone designed to be the iPhone killer. Everyone, including the company, bought into the notion—that is, until the Note 7 began to literally explode. Its replacement model failed, too, and finally the company had to cancel the model altogether.

S&P 500 companies usually spend more money buying back shares when their stock prices are high, and less at the bottom end, according to Guru Focus, a Plano, Texas-based news, commentary, and publishing organization that tracks stock buybacks. Its research found that in the third quarter of 2007, S&P 500 companies spent more than $130 billion to buy back shares, which it turned out were at a market peak. By the first quarter of 2009, after the 2008 market collapse, market capitalization had shrunk to almost half of the third-quarter 2007 number, yet companies spent only $31 billion on stock buybacks.[3]

Fig. 3.3 Share Buybacks by S&P 500 Companies

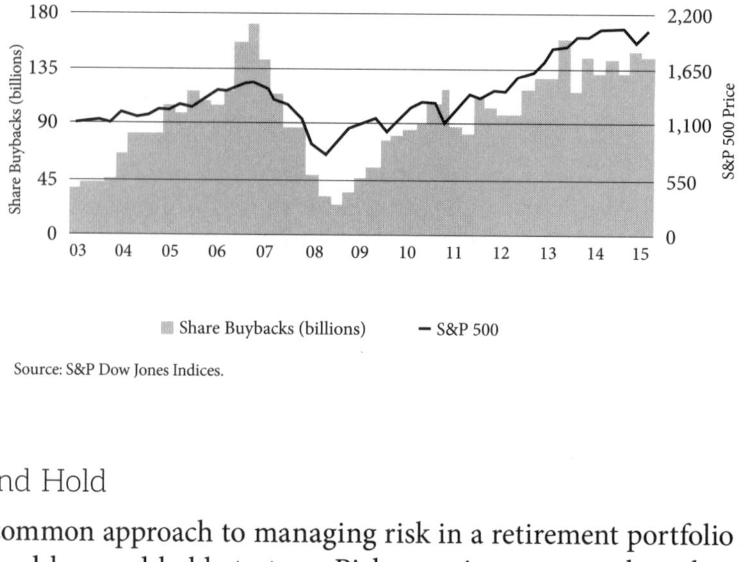

Source: S&P Dow Jones Indices.

Buy and Hold

A common approach to managing risk in a retirement portfolio is the traditional buy-and-hold strategy. Pick your investments, buy them, and then hold them until you're ready to retire. No muss, no fuss, and plenty of cash to live on for the rest of your life. Sound familiar?

For many, this is standard operating procedure for retirement portfolio investing. One big problem, however, is it's a seriously flawed strategy. Consider that the research regularly cited to support a buy-and-hold approach to retirement investing often relies on time lines of 50 to 70 years. That's time an individual investor usually doesn't have. The same research may use institutional investor models for its data, too. Unfortunately, neither provides rank-and-file investors a very accurate or valuable picture within the context of their portfolios.

Institutional investors have deeper pockets than individuals. They don't have to worry about reaching a certain point in the near future, shifting gears, and living off an investment. When we as individuals are investing for our retirement, such things matter. We simply can't afford the time or the losses.

The 2008 market collapse and its devastation on retirement portfolios was a wake-up call. What once worked for retirement investing rarely gets the job done anymore. You and your money can do better. That's what the New ROI is all about. It lays out a simple alternative that allows your money to grow within reasonable time frames, and without fear of devastating losses.

Blame the potential for losses with a buy-and-hold strategy on our roller-coaster markets and the economic and political uncertainties so prevalent today. Blame it on program trading, or blame something else. Your financial future isn't about laying blame. Instead, whatever you do, it's time to wake up to the reality that buy-and-hold is a flawed strategy, especially if you're near or already in retirement.

Fig. 3.4 New ROI Vs. S&P 500

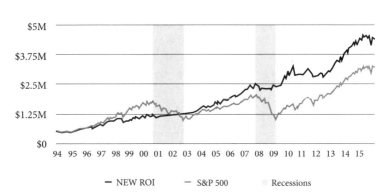

Data: Back-tested simulation January 1, 1994 through December 31, 2015.
S&P 500 data provided by Standard & Poor's.

Chasing Top Managers

Looking to stellar fund managers' past performance as a guarantee of future gains—long touted as a reliable marker for substantial returns—is not a solid approach to retirement investing, either. When the fine print in a prospectus says "Past performance is not indicative of future returns," it's best to recognize that upfront and pay attention to the warning.

Remember earlier when we discussed evolutionary biases that are human nature? They include everyone—financial professionals, too. You might think someone is above making biased choices because of his or her experience or certifications, but unless he or she has strict protocols that rely on mechanical models, emotions can creep into the decision-making process.

In 2009, Michael and Jane came to me for the first time after losing 58 percent of their savings in the Legg Mason Value Trust managed by Bill Miller. Bill is arguably the best mutual fund manager of his era. The fund, under Bill's management, outperformed the S&P 500 every year from 1991 to 2005. Unfortunately for Michael and Jane, though, that was the end of a great run. In 2006, the Legg Mason fund earned only 6 percent, before losing 6 percent in 2007, and then down a whopping 55 percent in 2008.

Just because a manager makes the right decisions one year or for several years isn't a guarantee of similar performance in subsequent years. The top 30 mutual funds returned 25.47 percent from 1991 to 2000, beating out gains of the S&P 500 by more than 6 percentage points. In the decade that followed, 2000 to 2010, the same funds earned less than 1 percent compared with the S&P 500's 2.84 percent gain. That's according to numbers calculated from the CRSP Survivor-Bias-Free Mutual Fund Database, provided courtesy of the University of Chicago on behalf of its Center for Research in Security Prices at Chicago Booth and Standard & Poor's Index Services Group.[4]

Chasing Top Performers

Yet another popular, albeit often flawed, approach to portfolio management involves chasing top performers—stocks that currently or in the recent past—provided stellar performance.

No matter the time span, chasing last year's winners—like chasing top managers—is often a losing proposition, according to the S&P 500 Persistence Scorecard. Out of nearly 700 domestic equity funds tracked from March 2013 to March 2015, only about 5 percent remained in the top quartile of performers year over year. Of the 2,730 actively managed equity funds in 2006, only 59 percent survived 10 years. Even worse, only 21 percent of those survivors outperformed their benchmarks. Fixed income managers didn't fare any better.[5]

**Fig 3.5 Equity Mutual Fund Track Record
(10 Years Ending 2015)**

Notes: Survivors are funds that were still in existence as of December 31, 2015. Non-survivors include funds that were either liquidated or merged. Outperformers are funds that survived and beat their respective benchmarks. Source: CRSP Survivor-Bias-Free US Mutual Fund Database.

The Devil in the Data

If you can't trust your own judgment, the once top performer, or top manager, then surely you can go straight to the numbers and rely on the data, right? Unfortunately, that's not always the case, either.

The problem with much of the data is that it can lie, even when it's provided by some of the oldest and seemingly most trustworthy organizations.

Back-Testing

Investors, advisors, fund managers, and strategists often look to the past to help determine the potential for a product's or strategy's future performance. This use of historical market data or simulations to analyze how an investment strategy, product, or vehicle will perform in the future is known as back-testing.

Markets go through many phases, environments, and circumstances over both short and long periods of time. The more a hypothesis is tested, the more variation in scenarios, and the more and better opportunities to understand how a strategy or investment will perform under a given set of circumstances.

In other words, solid and scientific back-testing provides potential investors ahead of time a detailed picture of what they may be buying and how it could fare in various economic situations.

The Time Conundrum

Time is important in back-testing. When looking at a sample, the time period should encompass a variety of market conditions: bull and bear runs, bubbles, protracted recessions—any market activity that could impact your data. To perform a test on one or even a few market conditions could render that data inconclusive or lead to false conclusions, leaving potential investors' money at grave risk.

Most people—including many investment professionals—don't realize that the typical five or even 10 years of an investment's performance data is not scientifically considered enough time to represent real life. It simply doesn't provide an accurate picture of risks and rewards in a statistically significant time frame.

Instead, a minimum 20 years of performance data is necessary to accurately show how a strategy or investment will perform across a broad spectrum of market conditions.

Figure 3.6 compares the performance of a hypothetical supposedly low-volatility equities portfolio with that of the S&P 500 across similar time frames. As you can see, a back-test that's too short in duration can dramatically skew the results. For example, across the shortest time frame (January 1, 2006 to December 31, 2010), the low-volatility portfolio well out-performed the S&P 500. But in three different additional scenarios, increasing the time frame led to varying numbers but similar results. Each time the S&P beat out the touted low-volatility portfolio.

Fig. 3.6 Dangers of Short Duration Testing

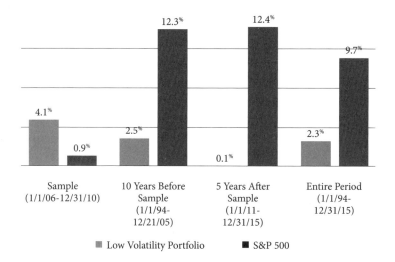

Understanding a Flawed Back-Test

Let's look closer at this hypothetical back-test for the so-called low volatility portfolio.

It's 2011, and we want to test what we think is a great low-volatility portfolio. We notice that when stock volatility spikes, the market heads southward quickly. We saw it happen in the bear market of 2008 and then again in the summer of 2010 and yet again in summer 2011.

So, we decide to back-test our strategy using as our barometer the VIX, a Chicago Board Options Exchange index that measures the volatility of the S&P 500. The rules are simple. If the VIX shows a reading greater than 15, we sell the S&P 500 and hold cash. If the VIX hits 15 or remains below that, we buy the S&P 500.

Looking over the years 2006 to 2010, our low volatility portfolio outperformed the S&P 500 by a substantial margin and with less volatility. Next, we decide to invest real money in our low-volatility system. Unfortunately, the next five-year period (2011 to 2015) did not fare as well. Our low-volatility portfolio barely broke even, while the S&P 500 averaged a gain of more than 12 percent.

If we had initially back-tested our theory over a longer time period, we would have found that the first five-year testing period (2006 to 2010) was an anomaly. The prior 12 years (1994 to 2005) actually showed a dramatic underperformance for what we initially considered a low-volatility portfolio.

Important Caveats of Back-Testing

As you can see, not all back-testing is equal. Applying the same investment strategy to a different time period can net different results, too, due to different macroeconomic risks.

Another important note: Not all back-testing is scientifically accurate. The right kind of back-testing—like the kind we do at Beacon Capital—should follow real scientific protocols and be reviewed by an independent third party, not the company promoting its own product. Otherwise, it can create a conflict of interest. Scientific back-testing is time-consuming and can be costlier, too. Unfortunately, not enough companies bother to do it right, and the data produced a tainted or inaccurate picture of a strategy or product's performance capabilities.

A true scientific, hypothetical back-test should meet the following criteria:

- 20-year test period to include various economic and market cycles, including bull and bear markets.

- Specific security selection and buy/sell rules that are applied and not changed throughout the test period.

- Timing of buy/sell rules is systematic and not changed throughout the test period.

- Specific holdings can be reproduced, along with criteria for inclusion or exclusion, as they changed throughout the test period.

- Timing and level of portfolios expenses, including trade expenses, are deducted to closely replicate live investment scenarios.

- Disclosures clearly stating that the results of the test period are hypothetical back-test results.

Misrepresenting Reality

It's important to read the fine print in marketing material and to question what you're being told by investing professionals, too. For instance, if a product's touted back-testing says one thing and an investment's actual returns show something entirely different, it should be cause for alarm.

That happened in 2012, when complaints surfaced about the market-leading active ETF management strategy, AlphaSector from Massachusetts-based F-Squared Investments. The equities investment strategy wasn't generating the advertised promised returns. Enough investors complained, and an SEC investigation ensued. Eventually the SEC charged that F-Squared had defrauded investors with performance data exaggerated by as much as 350 percent.

In 2014, the company agreed to pay $35 million and admit wrongdoing to settle claims. A number of firms that traded its product faced scrutiny as a result.[6]

Fallout from the F-Squared fraud may not be over yet, either. In August 2016, the SEC announced penalties against 13 investment advisory firms that promoted F-Squared's AlphaSector, claiming the firms didn't do enough to verify the accuracy of F-Squared's claims.[7]

Amiss With Factor Investing

Not all bad back-testing—overfitting—is necessarily fraudulent. But it can give investors a false sense of security at the cost of future retirement security.

That has happened in many cases with a hot equities trend today: factor investing. The approach calls for investors to buy small capitalization companies with a value tilt. That is, invest in a smaller public company with a capitalization of about $300 million to $2 billion with its stock that is relatively inexpensive compared with its fundamentals and that generally provides a good dividend.

The basic premise is that, over time, these smaller companies offer better returns. They do, but only over very long periods of time. It's the same as with the stock market. Since 1928, over time it's performed very well in terms of where it began and where it is today.

**Fig 3.7 S&P 500 vs. Small Cap
Value Stocks**

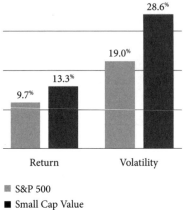

Return   Volatility

■ S&P 500
■ Small Cap Value

Notes: Volatility is measured by annualized standard deviation.
Source: Dimensional Fund Advisors.
Data: 1928-2015.

The problem, of course, lies with what happens in between the beginning and today—the lows and the highs, and the roller-coaster ride with its potential for big losses. What the experts and people touting these small caps usually downplay is the reason why the small-cap value stocks do better. The answer is that they are higher risk and therefore should generate a higher return over time. It's the same with large-company (large-cap) stocks that have the potential to generate a better return than government bonds over long time periods. Higher risk means the potential for greater returns as well as greater losses. As with any other investment, buyers willing to gamble on the risk expect to be compensated in the form of better returns.

Small-cap value stocks have outpaced the S&P 500 over the long haul. From 1928 to 2015, small caps have yielded 13.3 percent compared with 9.7 percent for the S&P 500. But in the interim, the small caps were much more volatile—more than a third more volatile; hence an investor's money was at greater risk.

Last Words

Let's review some of the essentials discussed in this chapter:

- When it comes to any kind of investing, the fact that everyone else is doing it certainly doesn't always translate to long-term investment success.

- No one has a crystal ball that can accurately predict what markets will do in the future.

- That "deal of a lifetime" likely isn't. And, you're probably too late to get in on the win anyway.

- Get the emotion out of your investing decisions. If you don't, there's a good chance your portfolio will suffer.

- Successful investing is *not* about riding the latest hot ticket to the top. Remember: Bubbles—no matter in what industry or sector—eventually burst, and often result in devastated portfolios.

- Forget market timing. If the experts can't do it successfully, the chances of you doing it aren't too good, either.

- The data can lie. As difficult as this is to believe, the data that many experts use to determine the potential for the future success of an investment or strategy aren't always truthful.

- The use of historical market data or simulations to analyze future performance is known as back-testing.

- Markets go through many different phases and changes over the short and long term. Therefore, the more you know the hypothetical variations that an investment or strategy is exposed to, the clearer will be your understanding of how the strategy or investment will perform under a given set of circumstances.

- For a back-test to be a scientifically accurate reflection of how an investment will perform under varying conditions, it requires a minimum 20-year test scenario.

- Many back-tests don't cover long-enough time frames, and can mislead or even defraud potential investors.

Now It's Your Turn

To help you take control of your equities investing portfolio with the New ROI in mind, some questions to ask yourself about your investing, portfolio, and financial future include:

- Have you ever picked up a hot stock or investment tip, and acted on it? It could be a tip from family, friend, even a media guru.

- What was the result? Did you come out way ahead, break even, or end up way behind? Too often, that hot tip isn't, and your retirement portfolio can suffer dramatically.

- Have you or your advisor ever tried to time the market—buy in at the low point and sell at the high point, for example? If so, did you succeed? Did you come out ahead? Not many people do. Whatever the result, though, hopefully you recognized that it's not that easy, even for the experts.

- Do any of your current investments provide back-testing as proof of performance? Does the back-testing meet the requirements for a scientific, hypothetical back-test? A few of those requirements include 20-year test period, specific rules and regulations applied throughout the entire period, and clearly stated disclosures.

- How much money have you let slip out of your portfolio because of a buy-and-hold strategy? Too many people end up subscribing to buy and hold as their approach to retirement investing. That doesn't allow your money to capitalize on market upsides or protect it against potential losses on the downside.

4 Maintain Discipline: Get the Emotion Out and Watch Your Portfolio Grow

EMOTIONS HAVE NO PLACE in investment decision-making. When personal biases are allowed to creep into investing decisions, the financial results can be catastrophic. That sounds harsh, but the financial crisis of 2008 is just one example of a horrific market fallout that crushed nest eggs, postponed retirement plans, and even brought people out of retirement in efforts to rebuild finances.

That's why in times of economic and emotional turmoil and stress, the savvy investor doesn't ask, "What should I do with my investments now?" or "Who should I ask for advice?" Instead, he or she already has a portfolio management strategy in place that cuts emotions from the equation.

When it comes to the equity portion of your portfolio, the "New ROI" does just that by laying out in advance a set of strict ground rules based on sound investing fundamentals and science based on decades of proven results. Those rules spell out what moves to make, when to make them, and how those triggers will be pulled. Nothing is left to chance or whims. That in turn can eliminate the uncertainty and fear associated with our culture's day-to-day, week-to-week, and month-to-month political and economic turmoil, and the dramatic market swings that often result.

With the right strategy—the New ROI—in place, you and your money can relax no matter what's happening around you, comfortable in the knowledge that your nest egg has the essential opportunity to grow, capitalizing on market upswings, while it's also protected from potential disaster.

The Ups and Downs of Fear and Greed

Do you jump at the latest market trend or the hottest stock tip? Or do you fall into that other category, and avoid equity investing altogether? Either path can prevent you from reaching your retirement goals. Whether greed or fear rules your investment decisions, you are allowing emotions to run your plans rather than allowing a mechanical-based model to steer your course.

Election's Real Winners

And in case you think that only individual investors are prone to emotional financial decisions, think again.

Think about November 8, 2016, the night of the U.S. presidential elections. Resoundingly, political pollsters had predicted a Hilary Clinton victory. That prediction had carried over to the financial markets, where the professionals had anticipated and taken actions with their investments based on a Clinton victory. When it became apparent that Trump would win, the markets panicked. The Dow Jones Industrial Average dropped 827 points in after-hours trading. Futures for the S&P 500 initially dropped 4 percent.

Had the election results occurred during the heat of a trading day, investors would have seen huge losses, but because all of this happened after hours, investors had time to cool off and get control of their emotions by the opening bell the next morning.

Many investors may have attributed their escape from losses that night to luck. I prefer to approach investing with sound fundamentals and mechanical models. Because of that philosophy, on election night, as markets yo-yoed from one end of the spectrum to the other, my holdings and those of our clients were secure. It didn't matter who won the election; we had the same plan in place regardless of a Trump or Clinton victory. The real winners that night were our clients whose investments weren't affected by the recklessness of human emotions.

The Emotions Factor

Anyone—whether an individual investor or professional equities trader—can fall prey to emotion-driven erratic behavior unless he or she has in place a mechanical model in their investing. That's a set of pre-determined rules for investing that are followed no matter what.

Emotional creep in part is why passive indexes do better year over year than actively managed ones. It also contributes to the dismal performance record of individual investors when it comes to picking stocks, timing markets, or trying to buy low and sell high.

If terrorists bomb an oil pipeline in Saudi Arabia or the chairman of the Federal Reserve dangles the idea of raising interest rates, 24/7 media outlets jump on the news, and investors and money managers notice. They make buy/sell moves and markets react, generally not in a favorable direction.

Once a sell-off begins, it often can steamroll, also driven by various emotions, including fear, and the herd mentality that fear can spark. After all, we all like to be winners. No wants to be left out of a good investment, or holding onto a bad one.

Fig. 4.1 Investing and Emotions

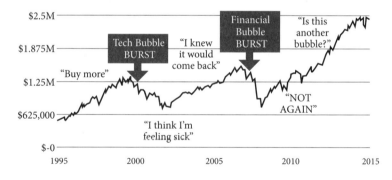

Source: Standard and Poor's.
Data: January 1, 1995 – December 31, 2015.

Falling markets evoke the emotion of fear because of the perceived threat that markets will continue to fall. If a market is reacting to a specific external action like a terrorist attack or economic event, people may worry not only about their financial futures, but their personal security as well.

The natural bias or emotion associated with fear is to flee the source of the perceived threat—to get rid of, avoid, or sell off a holding or holdings, for example, which in turn will lead to relief and feeling better. It can be a false sense of security, however, because often a sell-off can mean taking a big loss on an investment.

Too Little/Too Late?

Similar moves and biases happen with market upsides, only in this case the bias is fueled by the emotion of greed. The market may start a run-up or be in the middle of a bubble like the dot-com craze in 2000 or the brief biotech fad of early 2015. Even though an investor may know biotech stocks are overvalued, greed takes center stage, and he or she sinks their money in anyway.

As I mentioned earlier, by the time you hear of a hot stock tip, the big gains likely already are past. All you can do is ride it out upward, and then downward. Rather than buy low and sell high, the reality is people end up buying high and selling low.

In the last chapter, you heard the tale of the couple, Melina, the pharmacy tech, and her teacher husband, Mark. The two were biotech happy in early 2015. Even though they saw friends lose big when the dot-com bubble burst in 2000, and more friends lose their retirement savings in 2008, their emotions took over when biotech began its climb. They knew better than to invest their nest egg heavily in stock from AVEO, the company where Melina worked. But that didn't stop them.

As is typical when emotions rule, Melina and Mark rationalized that this time around, things were different. This wasn't a bubble; this was a real and logical increase in the value of biotech companies, and they intended to capitalize on it. Plus, they were talking about stock in the company where Melina had worked for years, so nothing bad would happen. Right?

Fig. 4.2 AVEO Pharmaceuticals

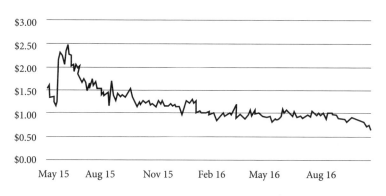

Source: www.finance.yahoo.com.

Wrong. Emotions beat out logic and rational thinking. When the bio-tech bubble collapsed, the duo lost big. By the time it was over, they had lost much more than they could afford to lose. Now their retirement is on hold until, or if, they can rebuild their nest egg.

Such heady, emotion-led investing isn't limited to an industry bub-ble, either. The bottom can and does regularly drop out of all types of companies and commodities in all kinds of industries. All it takes is one precipitous—albeit even temporary—drop in an equity's price to anni-hilate years of a portfolio's gains.

A Better Alternative

Given the uncertainties in today's political and economic environment, and the potential negative effect on a retirement portfolio, it's especially important for investors to make the necessary moves now to get the emo-tion out of their investment decision-making.

Not doing so can lead to disastrous portfolio performance results—in the short term or over the long haul. Whether over a one-year time span or 30 years, without a strict, rules-based portfolio management strategy in place, individuals can't get the emotion out of their investment decisions, and their investment returns often reflect that inability. Individuals simply end up making bad investor decisions at critical points, according to re-search from Dalbar, investor behavior experts.[1]

Fig. 4.3 Growth of $500,000 Investment

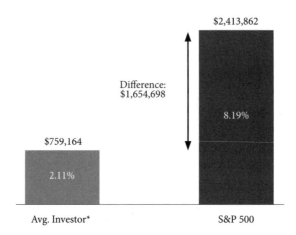

*Average asset allocation mutual fund investor.
Source: Dalbar. Data: 20-year period ending 12/31/2015.

Let's look at a $500,000 portfolio invested over a 20-year period ended December 31, 2015. The average mutual fund investor who relied on his or her own decision-making ended up with a portfolio worth $759,164. That compares with more than $2.4 million in the portfolio that simply mirrored the S&P 500, according to Dalbar's Quantitative Analysis of Investor Behavior 2016.[2]

Negative Economic Toll

More numerical evidence of the negative economic toll of investor bias comes from Dalbar. Their research shows that an average asset allocation investor—someone with a portfolio made up of a blend of stocks and bonds—earned just 2.1 percent from 1996 through 2015. That stacks up to be less than inflation, and far less than other benchmark indicators.[3]

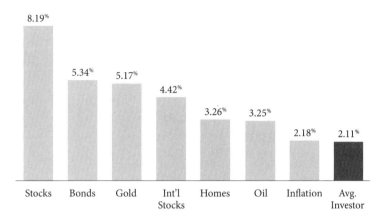

Fig 4.4 The Average Investor Underperforms

Source: Dalbar Inc.
Data: 20 year annualized returns (1996-2015).

Even the top money managers can and do suffer big losses as the result of conscious or subconscious emotion-led investment decisions. Wall Street is littered with that carnage.

The Science of Emotional Investing

Removing emotion from buying, selling, and holding sounds simple enough, but for the average investor, it's seldom easy.

To begin with, how we as humans react in various scenarios and when exposed to various stimuli is part of the pattern of human behavior. It's in our DNA. As investors, we may like to think of what we do and how we act under certain circumstances as unique, of our own making, and because of our wisdom and decision-making prowess. Though sometimes our actions may involve a degree of individual choice, those investment moves generally aren't unique or bias-free, unemotional responses. Rather, our actions are typically human responses based on a given set of external circumstances.

Believe it or not, investors often act irrationally, too, when making their money decisions. Even though plenty of information is available, emotions lead investors to make snap—often, wrong—decisions, even when they know better.

Emotion-driven investing isn't a new phenomenon. Thomas Gibson studied and wrote about it in his 1922 investment classic, *The Facts About Speculation*. After analyzing 4,000 investment accounts—a large number for his era—Gibson concluded, "The most glaringly apparent cause of loss... was the almost universal habit of making purchases at high prices after a material rise had already occurred. This error is of a wholly psychological character."[4]

Patterns of Behavior

Behavioral finance delves into the irrational behavior that can accompany investing. This science-based field examines theories from the areas of psychology and finance to better identify and understand the actions of investors in conjunction with the movements of markets.

Behavioral finance allows us to analyze how investors behave under various circumstances, so we can better understand and even try to modify some of these less-than-ideal behaviors from an investing and savings standpoint.

Empirical Evidence

The field of behavioral finance gained prominence after Daniel Kahneman and Vernon L. Smith shared the Nobel Prize in Economic Sciences in 2002. Since then, an entire industry has emerged with popular books, annual conferences, and documentary films all touting breakthroughs in the field and what its study can tell us about the link between our own psychology and the financial decisions we make.

The bottom line is that our biases are ingrained. That's one more reason to utilize mechanical-based models.

The Peter Lynch Phenomenon

Human emotions drive bad investment decisions of even the most expert investors among us. That's whether the buy, sell, or hold is in reaction to news, market movements, trends, economic theories, or "gut feelings" and other personal decisions.

We have a choice as investors: We can take the necessary steps and embrace specific rules to remove our biases. Otherwise, as behavioral finance demonstrates, it's inevitable that we will derail even the best-laid and best-intended investment plans.

An older example of the individual investor error involves Peter Lynch, who famously managed Fidelity Magellan Fund in the 1980s. During his tenure, Lynch brought the fund fantastic returns, beating the S&P 500 every year that he managed the fund and it was open to the public. But the average Fidelity Magellan investor didn't earn nearly as much as Lynch or the fund itself.

That's because rather than leave the big wins up to Lynch, those individual investors figured they could outthink him. They tried to anticipate and capitalize on what they thought Lynch planned to do. Generally, those investors ended up selling at the wrong time. Without Lynch's self-imposed set of rules, investing in or selling shares in the fund became an emotional gamble.

Looking at the numbers, from 1981 to 1990, the fund earned 21.8 percent, beating out the S&P 500, which earned only 16.2 percent. But, the average Fidelity Magellan investor earned only 13.4 percent.[5]

**Fig 4.5 Fidelity Magellan vs.
Fidelity Magellan Investors**

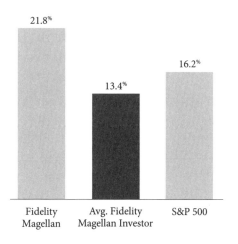

Source: www.cbsnews.com. "Lessons From a Great
Fund Manager's Record". July 16, 2010.

No one questioned Lynch's investing prowess, but the only person who knew what Lynch was going to do with an investment was Lynch. That's known as a black box strategy. The downside with that approach is an investor doesn't know what's inside the box—what to expect or do in an external event—and inevitably emotions take over.

When markets became volatile, fund investors didn't know if or when Lynch would move to protect their holdings, so those investors took control and sold the holdings themselves. It was emotional selling triggered by the fear associated with the unknown. Investors' portfolios paid the price of their emotional investment decisions.

Ultimately, as the Fidelity Magellan numbers so aptly demonstrate, emotions—consciously or not—tend to skew lower overall portfolio returns because of how people feel about gains and losses. That brings in yet another human trait known as cognitive bias. I'll talk more about that later.

The Luster of Safe Havens

Emotions also send investors to safe havens, especially in times of economic and political turmoil. Typically, we hear about the importance of a safe haven for our money in the context of more conservative—therefore *safe*—investments as we near retirement. Usually that means fixed-rate investment options like certificates of deposits or Treasuries, which barely keep up with inflation, and bonds or annuities.

Temporary Matters

The New ROI strategy for equity investing, with its stop-loss tenet, occasionally requires a temporary use of safe havens in the event of extreme market volatility—a 10-percent drop in the S&P 500. The key word, however, is *temporary*. It's only for the short term until markets recover enough to re-enter.

On the other hand, plenty of investment organizations tout their safe-haven products as ongoing and permanent investments for your money.

In today's low interest-rate environment and with today's market volatilities and the rising costs of inflation, looking to safe havens as a long-term investing strategy generally can't generate the growth required to build a portfolio with future reliability of retirement income in mind.

Gold's Allure

In times of recession and unrest, we often hear people making the big pronouncement "Now is the time to buy gold." Historically, the metal has been considered by many to be the ultimate safe haven—a hard asset people clamor for and because it historically retained its value in economically perilous times.

That's not exactly true today. Just in the last year—October 2015 to October 2016—prices per ounce of the precious metal have seesawed up to as high as $1,368.30 in early August 2016, and down to as low as $1,052.80 in mid-December 2015—a variation of more than 23 percent. During the last recession, when financial markets collapsed in 2008, emotions predictably led to a modern-day gold rush. During the 2008 to 2009 period, gold climbed to as high as $984.10 an ounce in March 2008 and fell to as low as $732.96 an ounce by November that year—a greater than 25 percent change.[6]

Fig. 4.6 Gold Prices

Source: www.apmex.com/spotprices/gold-price.
Data: January 3, 2008 – September 310, 2016.

An Emotional Red Flag

A few years ago, at the height of the Great Recession, we were bombarded with advertisements to buy or sell gold. The message was everywhere: on television, the Internet, in newspapers and magazines, and even on billboards. Before that latest gold buzz, it was real estate as the ultimate money-maker—for zero money down, an easy flip, and quick cash in your pocket.

Those ads that bombard us and play on our emotions are a great barometer of the extent of a bubble and/or the perception of the current rate of inflation, an impending recession, or a crashing economy. When they flood the airwaves or our mind space, that's usually a sign the bubble is destined to burst, and sooner rather than later.

Simple Reasoning Leads to Solid Solution

The takeaway, though, is that no matter the investment in a perceived safe haven—whether a bar of gold, a designated conservative fixed-income vehicle, a favorite equity, or something else—in today's economy nothing seems immune to the ups and downs of drastic market swings.

Instead of often financially debilitating decisions made in the heat of the moment, investors need to build protections into their portfolios so they're prepared, no matter what transpires with markets, politics, or the economy.

With the New ROI, rather than having emotions dictating investment moves, scientifically derived investing rules do the work. That's what a truly successful retirement investing system aimed at reliability of income is all about.

Rules-Based Investing

The reason a passive index like the S&P 500 beats out individual investors and most investment managers is that it has rules in place and never deviates from them. Those rules create a plan to insulate the index from the inevitable and unavoidable emotional aspects that go with personal/human-based decision-making.

The S&P 500 is a weighted index based on the market capitalization of its participating companies. That weighting is regularly readjusted as company market capitalizations change—no exceptions, and no deviations from that formula.

Individual investors, on the other hand, are always changing their minds, shuffling investments, chasing various hot investing philosophies of the moment, and pursuing their personal preferences. It's simply a part of our human nature; it's the behavioral finance aspect of investing. And it's still more reason to consider an alternative that doesn't try to predict what markets will or won't do, when, or why.

Instead, to give your money a fighting chance to grow amid dramatic market swings today demands both an active and a passive approach to investing.

The Index Fallacy

Simply tracking a passive index isn't enough to protect your money from economic variables.

Instead, the solution is an approach to investing that, like an index, relies on a specific set of rules—rules to be adhered to and followed day in and day out. But, unlike an index, this rules-based approach comes with active built-in protections against dramatic losses that often are unrecoverable within realistic time frames.

Backed by Science

Too often, people see investing in the abstract rather than for what it is: a science. It's that science, not emotion, that provides the best, most reliable road to retirement investing success. When properly applied—through the New ROI equity management strategy—investors can give their money the opportunities and protections it needs to build a portfolio for the future.

We rely on rules that spell out how to manage a stock portfolio. This isn't about persuading you to trust a theory or a company. The New ROI is based on mathematical principles that don't change and are the result of long-term—more than 20 years—of mathematically back-tested data that follows strict scientific protocols.

Robo's Unreliability

This isn't automatic or robo-investing. Robo-advisors, online systems, and robo-investing software rely on computer algorithms to automate and manage a portfolio. That takes the emotion out, but the approach generally falls apart later.

A portfolio may start off with the right allocations, but as markets and economics change, the portfolio's allocations and adjustments usually don't. Or, if they do, it's often very sporadic and not with an individual investor's needs in mind. As an investor ages, for example, a robo-portfolio may be re-allocated or readjusted to reflect a more conservative approach in terms of percentages of stocks or bonds. But those robo-approaches don't make changes based on the risk level of what's happening day in and day out in the world, in industries, and in the markets.

Robo-investing then becomes just another new-fangled iteration of the old buy-and-hold strategy.

With a robo-directed portfolio, you probably wouldn't know what or when, or even if you need to sell or readjust your holdings because the market is crashing, and you certainly wouldn't be notified to pull your money out of that investment for protection.

Robo-investing simply is not a reliable guarantee that your portfolio will generate the earnings it needs while providing diversity and protections to survive the downturns, and eventually provide a reliable income in retirement.

Last Words

Let's review some of the essentials discussed in this chapter:

- The New ROI lays out a set of strict mechanical-based rules that stick to strong investing fundamentals and science and does not deviate due to emotions or whims.

- Adherence to those ground rules is essential to long-term investing success with the goal of reliability of income in retirement.

- The emotions of fear and greed drive investment decision-making for the clear majority of individuals, professionals, and experts. Those emotions can interfere with rational thinking, too.

- The herd mentality can exacerbate market downturns. Investors become fearful of the perceived threat that markets are collapsing.

- That same mentality can fuel market run-ups and subsequent bubbles. This time, however, the driving emotion is greed.

- The solution to successful retirement investing hinges on getting the emotion out of investment decision-making.

- Behavioral finance is a science that combines psychology and finance to help understand and explain investor behavior.

Now It's Your Turn

To help you take control of your investing portfolio with the New ROI in mind, some questions to ask yourself about your investing, portfolio, and financial future include:

- Do your emotions figure into your investing decisions? If so, what was the result of the last investment decision you made? Are you hanging on to that investment from your parents' estate that's only performing so-so? If you are, that's about emotions, not future retirement security. Your money deserves a better chance to grow.

- After major political or economic turmoil, have you ever called your financial advisor for reassurance? Once again, that's about emotion-led investment decision making.

- Have you ever impulsively bought or sold—or wanted to buy or sell—an investment during or as the result of an economic-related occurrence (dropping interest rates, for example, or a terrorist attack somewhere)? If so, again, that's a result of your emotions leading the charge.

- Do you lose sleep at night over your investments, especially in times of economic and political turmoil and terrorism? You don't have to, and you shouldn't if you take a rules-based approach to investing, and have built-in protections against devastating losses.

5 Your Portfolio: The Right Mix of Equities and Bonds

NOW THAT YOU better recognize the importance of effective risk management with equity investing today, it's time to broaden our scope and take a comprehensive view of your retirement portfolio.

Putting together a complete retirement portfolio tailored for your future goes well beyond buying a series of equities and figuring you're set for life. You need to ask yourself a few questions:

Where am I in my investment cycle?

How diversified are my holdings?

What is my risk tolerance?

Does my risk tolerance match my current holdings?

These are important questions to answer before you make any additional investments. They're also a great launching point for you to incorporate the "New ROI" as the basis for your investment plan and strike the mix of investments that is right for you.

Balancing Act

Bonds (investment grade) offer your portfolio stability with regular guaranteed returns—albeit low returns given our low interest-rate environment. Equities, on the other hand, are the wild card and provide the opportunity your money needs to grow today to meet your needs tomorrow.

Both, combined correctly, can work in tandem to your long-range financial advantage. Stocks power your portfolio's growth so that it can prosper. Bonds act as the safety net in the event the market tumbles or catastrophe happens. Keep in mind that generally, bonds move inversely to interest rates.

An easy way to explain the stocks and bonds mix in a portfolio is a sailing analogy. The rules of the water require life preservers for everyone aboard the boat. It's a simple safety precaution ahead of time in case of catastrophe—the boat capsizes, for example, or someone goes overboard accidentally. It's a no-brainer. With a life jacket on, you may go under water briefly, but you won't stay under for long, and chances are you'll be fine because you took precautions to save your life.

In investing, the life jackets are your portfolio's high-quality bonds. They help to protect some of your assets in the event of a market catastrophe. Let's look more closely at the role bonds can play and how you can know what's the best allocation of stocks and bonds in your portfolio.

Total Approach

Investors preparing today for financial security tomorrow must take the perspective of total return in building their retirement portfolio. Rather than focusing on the traditional return on investment—how much one stock or bond goes up or down—reliability of income in retirement demands a big-picture approach.

Everything from earnings and dividends, to costs, fees, taxes, and losses all add up to determine whether a retirement portfolio can provide enough income to meet your needs later.

Income, Growth, and Precautions

The best way to generate enough portfolio income is through capital gains from the stock side of a portfolio. However, as soon as you expose your portfolio to stocks, you expose your capital to downside risk. That's why stop-loss is important on the equity side.

But, with the big picture in mind, you also can maximize the protections in your retirement portfolio with the addition of bonds.

The Bond Advantage

Traditionally, in the days of double-digit interest rates, bonds could generate a comfortable income. Therefore, that often was their primary goal in a portfolio.

In our much-lower interest-rate environment today, that approach no longer satisfies necessary nest egg growth for a comfortable retirement. Instead, the primary focus for bonds today is the safety and the protection of your capital.

When markets fall, bonds typically do very well. At the very least, even if the price to purchase new bonds falls slightly, those already purchased bonds maintain their same income-producing levels. That's because when you buy a bond, you're buying its issuer's obligation to pay a specified amount regularly and to repay the bond's principal at its maturity. Even if bond prices don't recover, the bonds still generate the same income stream.

Those bonds in a portfolio in turn can help offset potential equity losses. With the "New ROI" strategy, equity losses are limited by stop-loss, so the addition of bonds further works to insulate your money from serious loss.

The Effects of Volatility

Of course, with today's market volatility, even bonds don't always behave as traditionally expected. When interest rates increased in December 2015, despite historical precedent to the contrary, bond prices didn't drop as investors would expect.

Instead, the extreme volatility in markets in early 2016 actually pushed bonds higher as investors' emotions prompted a flight to conservative safe havens. Bonds top that list of safe places.

So much for predicting market movements and keeping emotions out of investment decisions.

Risk Tolerance and Your Portfolio

How a portfolio is allocated is usually determined by risk tolerance "quizzes" or by time horizon as in age and withdrawal needs. Whatever your risk preferences, you'll likely make better investment decisions if you understand upfront your personal comfort levels and what makes the most sense when it comes to investing your money.

If you address portfolio allocation in that manner—either with an advisor's help or on your own—you're one step closer to getting the emotion out of the investing equation.

For example, if you're strongly risk averse (very conservative in your risk tolerance) and you decide to invest your entire portfolio in equities (higher risk/potential for greater gains), even with a built-in stop-loss strategy, you'll likely always be worried about your investments. Instead, perhaps a 70-percent bonds/30-percent stock mix (less risk/less potential for gains) might better fit your age and risk profile.

In short, the bonds provide more portfolio stability to offset the greater risk—albeit limited with stop-loss protections—of stocks. A heavily weighted bond portfolio doesn't have the growth potential of an equity-weighted portfolio. But it offers you better peace of mind, and, with the New ROI approach, such a portfolio can have built-in protections against losses.

Beyond the Typical

Most advisors, experts, and traditional portfolio models break risk tolerance levels into three different portfolios: aggressive (the highest risk), balanced (midstream), and conservative (the least risk). Traditionally that's meant a portfolio breakdown that includes:

- **Aggressive.** Portfolio allocation: 100 percent stocks, essentially mirroring the S&P 500.

- **Balanced.** Portfolio allocation: 60 percent stocks and 40 percent bonds.

- **Conservative.** Portfolio allocation: 20 percent stocks and 80 percent bonds.

If this is the approach you prefer, it's important at the very least to adopt the New ROI mantra of making sure equities in your portfolio are divided by equal allocation across all 11 sectors.

A New Approach for the New ROI

Traditionally, this is the point in most retirement investing books or on the various how-to road maps at which you are presented with a risk tolerance quiz or a series of questions to answer that, when the results are tallied, miraculously gives you a clear picture of your risk tolerance level. That quiz result then sets the stage for your investing. Your future income reliability hinges on how you answer a few questions.

However, during my years in this business, I've learned to recognize that risk tolerance quizzes are *not* the best measure of your risk tolerance level—that amount of your money you're willing to risk while still being able to sleep well at night. To begin with, individuals often tend to answer quiz questions with a recent investing bias that doesn't really reflect their personal concerns. When stocks are doing well, they also tend to be aggressive in their risk tolerance; when stocks do poorly, they shift to a conservative bent. So, I've come up with an alternative New ROI approach to portfolio allocation.

No investor wants to lose money. That's a given. Another given is that, in today's volatile investing climate, retirees and soon-to-be retirees should invest as conservatively as possible to achieve their primary goal of generating a reliable income for life.

To that end, we've done the math and determined the optimal portfolio split to meet an investor's needs over his or her lifetime. Our model makes three assumptions in addition to the desire to not run out of money in one's lifetime:

1. Investors follow the New ROI strategy.

2. The portfolio mix is based on a life expectancy of age 100. You may not live that long, but what happens if you do? No one wants to run out of money in his or her lifetime.

3. The withdrawal rates stated are *safe*—a 98-percent probability of not running out of money.

Fig. 5.1 Recommended New ROI Stock Allocation

Age	Stock Allocation		
	4.0% Income	4.5% Income	5.0% Income
65	94%	*	*
66	86%	*	*
67	79%	*	*
68	72%	*	*
69	65%	*	*
70	58%	*	*
71	52%	97%	*
72	46%	87%	*
73	40%	78%	*
74	35%	69%	*
75	30%	61%	98%
76	25%	53%	86%
77	20%	45%	75%
78	16%	38%	65%
79	12%	32%	56%
80	9%	26%	47%
81	6%	20%	39%
82	3%	15%	31%
83	0%	10%	24%
84	0%	6%	18%
85	0%	2%	12%
86	0%	0%	7%
87	0%	0%	2%
88-100	0%	0%	0%

* This level of income is not sustainable to age 100.
Assumptions: Life expectancy is age 100. Income is increased annually by 3%. Objective is to have at least $1 left at age 100 with a 98% probability.

Typical retirement planning assumes that an individual needs to withdraw about 4 percent per year from a retirement portfolio to live comfortably and not run out of money over a 30-year retirement. That's whether your pre-retirement income is $100,000 or $5 million.

But things have changed in terms of life expectancies, lifestyles, and costs. That number has dropped closer to 3-percent withdrawal rates for the typical portfolio without the New ROI. That's scary, and a signal that many people could and likely will run out of money before they die.

With the New ROI, if you have a $100,000 portfolio and need to withdraw 4 percent per year for your living expenses, increasing every year to meet financial needs, you could start off very aggressively in your portfolio allocation—94 percent equities and 6 percent bonds—and not run out of money in your lifetime. Then, as you grow older, gradually you can shift your portfolio's weight more toward bonds (as indicated in Figure 5.1).

Looking at Figure 5.1, find your age in column one and then the percentage income withdrawal in the subsequent columns to determine stock allocation in your portfolio to meet your income growth and future withdrawal needs.

If, for example, you think you'll need 4.5-percent annual withdrawals at age 65 to meet your income needs, you'll find that combination of numbers doesn't work. It's not safe and not financially viable, according to our calculations. If you don't cut your expenses and still insist on withdrawing 4.5 percent a year, you may very well run out of money in your lifetime.

Getting it Done

Let's figure out step-by-step how to determine the optimal portfolio allocations for your personal situation. This is where the right advisor especially can help. I'll talk more about how later.

Cost of Retirement

First, you'll need to determine how much money you'll need to live on in retirement. Combined with your Social Security, how much money per month will it take to meet your lifestyle needs?

To calculate that amount, determine how much money you spend every month. Be sure to include discretionary spending as well as fixed expenses. You also should consider any annual expenses—property taxes, for example, as well as expected maintenance and repairs. What's the condition of your home's furnace, for example, or its roof?

Once you have calculated that number, then figure out if any of those expenses are likely to increase, decrease, or go away completely when you're no longer working and have retired. Wardrobe and daily transportation costs could decrease, but healthcare and leisure travel expenses could rise.

Be honest in your answers. Too often people think they'll spend less in retirement on entertainment—going out to dinner, for example—when in reality the entertainment tab frequently goes up because you end up with more time on your hands.

The old rule for the amount of money needed in retirement called for 70 percent of your pre-retirement income. If you earned $100,000 a year, that meant you would need $70,000 a year in retirement. But, again, things have changed.

Generally, I've found that the expenses change throughout retirement. Early in retirement expenses increase as retirees spend extra money doing all those things they always wanted to do, but didn't have the time. Then in mid-retirement, costs level out, and often decline somewhat as you've done most of the things you always wanted to do at this point, until they begin to rise again, usually because of added healthcare costs later in life.

Fig. 5.2 The Three Phases of Retirement

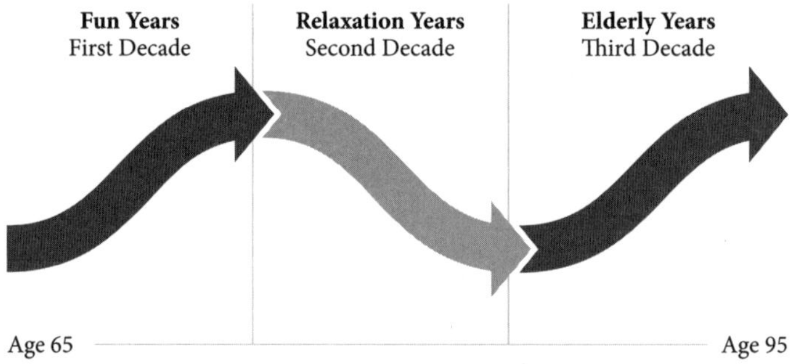

Fun Years
First Decade

Relaxation Years
Second Decade

Elderly Years
Third Decade

Age 65   Age 95

We Are All Different

There's no short-cut or simple way to figure out your financial needs in retirement. Everyone spends money differently. Working with an advisor—even short-term—can make this process much easier because he or she has experience with the nuances and details that most of us tend to overlook.

Once you have determined the amount of money you need, then estimate when you would like to retire and when it makes sense financially for you to do so. You can then look at Figure 5.1 to figure out the right portfolio allocation of stocks and bonds to meet your income needs.

You can periodically revisit the chart as you get older to readjust your portfolio's allocations to ensure that reliability of income in retirement.

The Takeaway

Now that you have a better idea how to align your portfolio allocations for optimal personal comfort, you can make better decisions to help ensure a comfortable financial future, along with current and ongoing peace of mind.

One size definitely does not fit all when it comes to investing for your retirement with future income reliability in mind. We are all different, as are our circumstances, risk comfort levels, and goals. Remember, too, those optimal allocations are fluid and can change over time.

Review Your Portfolio

Now let's look at your existing investment portfolio. How is it allocated in terms of stocks, bonds, and cash? Even if you've never thought about your portfolio in those terms, now is the time to take inventory.

Does your portfolio reflect the level of growth and risk that's optimal to meet your future reliability of income needs? If it does, great! You're one step closer to creating the right New ROI portfolio.

If your portfolio's investment mix doesn't match your needs, then it's time to readjust. No matter how small, those readjustments can make a difference in your overall daily comfort levels when it comes to investing. The right mix—combined with the ongoing safeguards of the New ROI approach to portfolio management—means less worry about today's uncertain economic times and market volatilities.

Last Words

Let's review some of the essentials discussed in this chapter:

- Your personal comfort level in terms of investment risk matters. Remember: No one size fits all when it comes to investing, retirement goals, or needs.

- Risk is fluid—both in terms of investments and personal risk exposure levels. Both change over time.

- Rather than the typical risk-tolerance-quiz approach to guide your portfolio allocations, we take a mathematical approach with the underlying premise that no one wants to lose money in the markets.

- Make sure to revisit your own risk tolerance comfort level every few years, especially if you start to worry about your investments. That's where talking to the right advisor can make a difference.

- Don't be afraid to make changes to your basic portfolio allocation as a result of changes in needs. Equal sector allocation doesn't change, but your portfolio's split between stocks and bonds likely will.

Now It's Your Turn

To help you take control of your investing portfolio with the New ROI in mind, some questions to ask yourself about your investing, portfolio, and financial future include:

- Do you lose sleep at night over your investments, especially in times of economic and political turmoil and terroristic threats? You don't have to, and you shouldn't if your portfolio is properly apportioned in accordance with your needs.

- Do you have bonds in your portfolio? Depending on your age, it makes sense to include some investment-grade bonds as security in the event markets drop.

- Have you given yourself realistic goals of what you want to accomplish with your retirement plan? And, do you have a plan that will realistically allow you to achieve those goals? That will be a great first step in developing your lifelong retirement plan.

Part

2 Equities: What to Do Now—
The "New ROI" Strategy

6 The Power of Losses

WHATEVER YOUR RISK tolerance or financial goals, one of the greatest challenges to saving and investing is the negative power of losses. A single loss can torpedo a portfolio and, with it, your hopes and dreams of a reliable income and financial security in retirement.

A loss, even when followed by gains, can wreak lasting havoc on your money. With the volatility of today's markets characterized by the all-too-frequent higher highs and lower lows, investors absolutely must pay attention to this very real, potentially catastrophic risk.

That's why long-term investing success isn't as much about winning big with that guaranteed *sure thing* or racking up every single gain possible as it is about learning how not to lose. That may sound counter-intuitive, but it's proven to be a successful path to consistently grow your portfolio.

That's also why a major tenet of the "New ROI" approach to equity portfolio management includes stop-loss provisions. If the S&P 500 drops by 10 percent, that's a signal to divest a portfolio's equity holdings and move them into a safe haven until markets recover. I'll talk more about that later.

The Double Whammy

Unfortunately, too few investors recognize the devastating power of losses, and thus leave their portfolios and financial futures vulnerable and unprotected. Let's look more closely at the crippling impact of losses.

When markets drop, a portfolio not only must deal with the actual loss—the result of the dropping value of the investments in the portfolio—but with the decreased core value of the overall portfolio itself. What remains of the investments in the portfolio then must work harder and require extended time simply to return to a breakeven point. And that doesn't take into account any investment/portfolio growth requirements to fund future needs.

If at the time of the initial loss, you're already in retirement and/or withdrawing funds regularly—to pay a child's or grandchild's education expenses, for example—then the struggle to rebuild your portfolio becomes that much more difficult. Just as with losses, these drawdowns shrink your core investment's value and force it to work harder to recover.

The road to financial recovery is steep, too. If an investment loses half its value, it takes much more than a 50-percent gain to return to initial levels. In fact, a market that's off 50 percent requires a 100 percent gain to return to break even.

Fig 6.1 Percentage Gain Needed to Recover From Loss

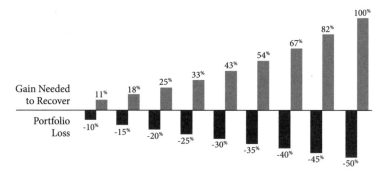

Roller-Coaster Markets

By now you have a clearer picture of today's new investing normal: roller-coaster markets that continually race up and down. That reality further stresses the ability of a portfolio to recover from a loss. Remember earlier the chart of the graceful, albeit misleading, portfolio arc that showed a smooth road into and through retirement (Figure. 1.4)?

Keep in mind that the typical retirement portfolio made up of stocks and bonds may *average* an 8.7 percent return over time. But the route to achieving that average isn't a graceful arc or a straight line upward, either. In a down year, that same portfolio could lose 20 percent or more of its value.

That's one more reason all investors need to build into their portfolios adequate protections that give their money solid opportunities to capitalize on market gains and to recover from market losses.

Just how much volatility is the new norm? Consider that in less than one month (from January 1, 2016, through January 20, 2016), the S&P 500 Index was down 9 percent. That meant if on the first day of the year, your portfolio's value was $100,000, and it tracked the S&P 500, even before the end of the month your nest egg would have dropped to $91,000. And that's only the first month and the first big drop of the year. In case you think that was an isolated instance—perhaps only the markets adjusting to the new year—the S&P 500 went on to lose 6 percent in February, and then 5 percent later in June.

Though none of those losses was great enough to trigger a stop-loss with the New ROI approach, they do illustrate the rocky nature of equities investing today.

Remember, too, that an investment requires gains greater than the loss to return to break even without factoring in any expenses associated with an investment or demands in terms of payouts.

A Real Bear

In a prolonged bear market, the outlook for your nest egg, if unprotected, is even worse. Let's look at what happened to a typical portfolio that tracked the S&P during the last big bear market (2007 to 2009). Let's assume a portfolio's value hit $100,000 with the S&P's high on October 9, 2007.

By the time the S&P bottomed out March 9, 2009, that portfolio's value had dropped to $45,000—a 55-percent loss.

What was left in the portfolio then needed to grow 122 percent to regain its losses without ever taking into consideration gains necessary for an investor to meet his or her retirement-income goals. Following that loss, the S&P 500 took nearly five years (from October 9, 2007 to August 16, 2012) to get back to the pre-crash high.

If someone was retired and dependent on his or her portfolio for income—let's assume he or she was withdrawing 5 percent annually—the S&P 500-based portfolio would not have returned to breakeven as of July 31, 2016. Those are sobering numbers and frightening realities that must be considered with retirement investing strategies.

Incidentally, if that same portfolio had been invested utilizing the New ROI equities approach, even with the 5-percent annual withdrawals, its value would be up 33 percent.

Fig 6.2 S&P 500 Annual Returns

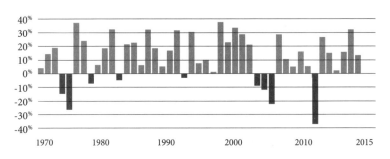

Source: Standard & Poor's Data: 1970-2015.

What if that decimated portfolio was yours, and you were 58 or 60 years old in 2008? Worse still, what if you had already retired? As I mentioned earlier, tens of thousands of Americans found out the hard way. The GAO estimates the losses from the 2008 market collapse at more than $10 trillion.[1] Losses could climb even higher when you factor in that many people today are still recovering.

On the other hand, if an investor had taken the New ROI approach with his or her portfolio, his or her holdings would have emerged from the bear in 2009 down only 5 percent, an amount that was quickly recovered. (See Figure 6.3.)

Fig 6.3 New ROI Portfolio vs. S&P 500

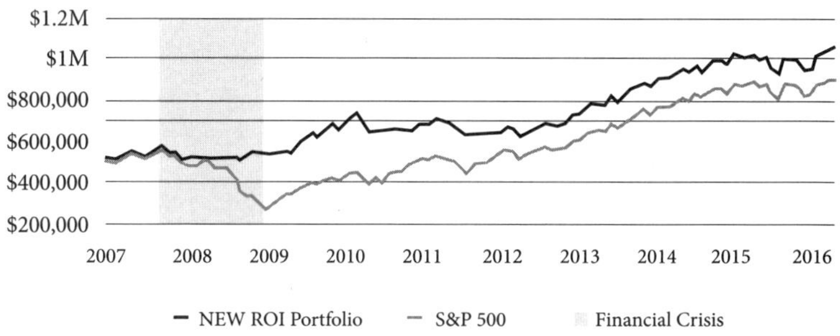

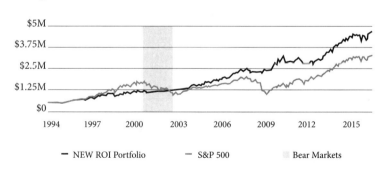

Data: Back-tested simulation January 1, 2007 – June 30, 2016.
S&P 500 data provided by Standard & Poor's.

Now let's track the performance of a New ROI portfolio and how it stacks up against the rise and fall of the S&P 500 over the same period. From 1994 to the end of the second quarter 2016, a $500,000 New ROI portfolio had grown to $4,708,326 as compared with just $3,304,268 for the portfolio that mirrored the S&P 500. Paying attention to potential exposure to losses in a portfolio, and taking precautions ahead of time, does make a big difference in your bottom line.

Fig. 6.4 New ROI Portfolio vs. S&P 500

Data: Back-tested simulation January 1, 1994 – June 30, 2016.
S&P 500 data provided by Standard & Poor's.

Decimated Portfolios

In case you think the crash of 2008–2009 didn't affect *that* many retirement investors' nest eggs, think again. In 2007, nearly 60 percent of all defined contribution retirement plans and IRA assets were in equities, according to the AARP's Public Policy Institute (PPI). Those assets lost 22 percent of their value, or about $2 trillion, in the 2008 market collapse. PPI estimated that older workers and retirees had 50 percent to 60 percent of their individual retirement savings in stocks, leaving many out of money and out of luck after the Great Recession.[2]

These very real numbers help us understand why, in part, so many older Americans have been forced to postpone retirement and why some who had already retired have had to return to the workforce to make ends meet.

History shows that recovering from these kinds of losses can take years, years that most investors simply don't have. As mentioned above, the S&P 500 climbed back to pre-crash levels by August 2012, but for those investors who lost so much, the power of losses took its toll.

Real Financial Tolls

At the beginning of 2008, Peter and Alice were looking forward to only one more year of working. Then, they planned to retire and do all those things they loved to do, but had put on hold while they built their nest egg. As of January 1, 2008, the couple had saved $500,000, which they had invested entirely in what they considered secure investments—funds that tracked the S&P 500. After all, markets go up over time; that's what everyone, including their financial advisor, always told them.

The couple planned to retire on December 31st that year, and then begin withdrawing 5 percent, or $25,000, a year from their portfolio. That money, plus their Social Security, would be plenty to live on because they owned their own home free and clear and had paid off all their other debts.

Then came the financial crisis and ultimately the market collapse that left the S&P 500 down 37 percent. Peter and Alice's $500,000 suddenly caved to $315,000 overnight. That meant their 5-percent annual withdrawals would to $15,744 instead of the expected $25,000. Factoring in their Social Security, perhaps they would have enough to live on but certainly not to pursue the activities they had long planned as part of their retirement.

Even if the couple had split their portfolio investments with 50 percent in the S&P 500 Index fund and 50 percent in a fund that mirrored the conservative Barclays Aggregate Bond Index, they would still have lost 17 percent of their nest egg. That less-crippling loss would raise their withdrawal to $20,826 annually.

On the other hand, if Peter and Alice had instead embraced the New ROI approach to managing their portfolio, the couple's capital would have remained intact after the collapse because they would have deployed a stop-loss when the market dropped 10 percent. So, rather than losing a big chunk of money, the portfolio would have ended 2008 up slightly—a 1.05-percent gain—and the couple could have retired on time and on track with a $505,237 nest egg.

Instead, Peter and Alice's original $500,000 S&P-invested portfolio didn't return to the breakeven point of $500,000 until February 29, 2012. (A portfolio split 50/50 between stocks and bonds would have regained its losses by March 31, 2010.) That meant the couple had to postpone retirement and keep working at minimum four additional years before they had enough in their nest egg to meet their retirement financial goals.

Adding to Peter and Alice's problems, the pair lost their financial confidence. They now constantly worry that another market collapse similar to that of 2008 could wipe out their savings and leave them vulnerable. That worry may haunt them the rest of their lives. In their case, the fear of running out of money in their lifetimes has become a very real possibility.

More Complications

For Peter and Alice and many others like them, losses take a psychological toll, too. It's behavioral finance again, and that cognitive bias known as loss aversion that I mentioned earlier.

In simple terms, we all hate to lose more than we like to win, so losses are twice as powerful as gains psychologically. If you doubt that, think about professional athletes who often say they like to win, but they *really* hate to lose even more.

In terms of investing, not only do losses cause more damage mathematically, but they also cause more damage psychologically. As an illustration, a 10-percent loss creates twice the pain that a 10-percent gain creates in terms of pleasure. That's why after big losses investors generally stay on the sidelines and take much longer to return to the market.

Fig. 6.5 Emotions of Gains and Losses

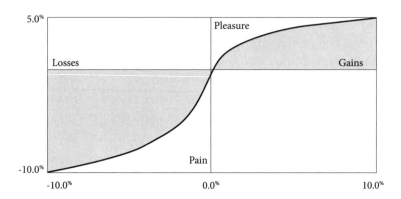

The Recovery Picture

After a loss, the road to recovery is a rough one. Financial expert Craig L. Israelsen, PhD, examined the length of time for a portfolio or investment to recover from a loss based on mathematical probabilities. Israelsen is a former professor of finance at Brigham Young University and now executive in residence at Woodbury School of Business, Utah Valley University.

He found that from 1970 to 2009, the S&P's largest one-year return was 37.58 percent in 1995. Thus, in 1995 it would have taken more than a year, even in the best of bull markets, to recover a 35-percent loss (similar to 2008). However, when you factor in the upward and downward trends characteristic of bear markets (and standard equity investing procedure these days), recovery becomes long and arduous.

Looking more closely at Israelsen's research, if a portfolio experienced a 10-percent loss, it still has only a 77.8-percent chance of complete recovery after five years. If it was a 20-percent loss, your money has only a little more than 72-percent chance it will have returned to breakeven after five years, according to the mathematical probabilities.[3]

Fig. 6.6 Probability of Recovery

Portfolio Loss	Gain Needed to Restore Loss	Percentage chance of recovery from loss within...					
		1 Year	2 Year	3 Year	4 Year	5 Year	10 Year
-10.0%	-11.1%	52.5%	74.4%	81.6%	78.4%	77.8%	93.5%
-20.0%	-25.0%	25.0%	48.7%	68.4%	67.6%	72.2%	93.5%
-35.0%	-54.0%	0.0%	17.9%	34.2%	56.8%	61.1%	93.5%
-50.0%	-100.0%	0.0%	0.0%	7.9%	13.5%	36.1%	80.6%
-65.0%	-186.0%	0.0%	0.0%	0.0%	2.7%	5.6%	61.3%

Source: "The Match of Gains and Losses," Craig L. Israelsen, Ph.D., Woodbury School of Business, Utah Valley University, 2010.

These numbers assume that no unusual or out-of-the-ordinary financial calamities befall markets in the interim. A glance at what have become the daily headlines on economic, political, and terror disruptions does much to dispel the assumption of a smooth road to recovery. The questions then become:

- Do you have the patience to wait 10 years or more simply to rebuild a devastated nest egg back to breakeven?

- Do you have the financial wherewithal to live on without having to tap into your nest egg at least until it returns to breakeven? Put plainly, can you afford to allow it to recover?

- What if recovery takes longer than a 10-year projection? Can you afford that?

We each must ask these questions and answer them realistically. After all, a goal of your investing for retirement is to build a portfolio and a financial future that can thrive and survive economic ups and downs. Not many people's portfolios can absorb that kind of a financial shock and then thrive. The onus is on you to make sure your portfolio is one of those built to last.

The Loss Momentum Effect

There are more negative impacts that a retirement portfolio must be prepared to cope with in the face of losses.

The momentum effect further threatens to eat into the chances your nest egg has to survive and thrive. When the market begins a downhill slide, often it's tough to find the footing to stop it. In other words, the momentum of the losses tends to push markets even lower. It's just like hiking on a muddy steep slope: Once you start to slip, it can be tough to regain your footing. The farther down you slide, the greater the momentum, and the faster you fall.

Analysis shows that a 10-percent market loss usually signals much bigger losses ahead. Consider what's happened historically when market losses surpassed the 10-percent mark:

- Since 1926, the stock market has dropped at least 10 percent a total of 29 times.

- In nearly half those instances (45 percent), before the slide was over, markets had dropped by more than 20 percent (20 percent is the marker that indicates a full bear market is under way).

- The median or most common loss that occurred once the markets passed the 10 percent loss was 19.35 percent.

- The average loss to markets was 27 percent.

Whether you're saving for retirement or something else, if, as an investor, you haven't prepared ahead of time for potential big downturns and have in place loss protections (like those the New ROI provides), these are tough losses to swallow. Often, it's too much for retirement portfolios to overcome even if only half a portfolio is invested in stocks.

Fig 6.7 Momentum of a 10% Loss

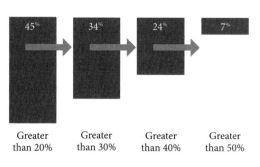

| Greater than 20% | Greater than 30% | Greater than 40% | Greater than 50% |

Source: Beacon Capital Management, Inc.
Data based on Dow Jones Industrial Average (1900-2015).

The Withdrawal Wrench in Your Plans

The problem of growing your retirement portfolio is exacerbated if for any reason you have to withdraw funds from your portfolio, especially if you're already retired and regularly counting on your nest egg for income.

Let's assume a retiree withdraws 6.5 percent annually from his or her portfolio. That's a scenario many retirement models say is possible. That means in the event of a 10-percent market drop, including the regular withdrawals, the effect on your portfolio equates to a 16.5-percent loss. Conversely, a 10-percent portfolio gain is really only a 3.5-percent gain. Factor in the daily ups and downs of markets, and that can make a portfolio's recovery a complex and lengthy process.

Fig 6.8 Withdrawals Weaken Gains and Magnify Losses

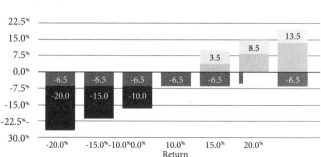

Adding to the Risk

The timing of a big market drop can further complicate your savings efforts and possibly torpedo your entire financial future. If that big market decline occurs in what we refer to as the "retirement risk zone," your nest egg is at even greater risk. The zone encompasses the last five years of savings and building your portfolio before retirement, and the first five years after you retire. In that time period, your assets are likely at their highest level and a slash in value can have a dramatic impact on your future retirement savings and earnings. To further complicate matters, a quarter of our population falls into that retirement risk zone, putting an enormous number of us in a position where they cannot afford to suffer a major loss.

Fig 6.9 Reliability of Income

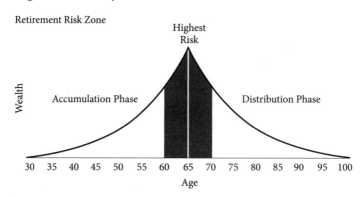

Tail Risk

When markets experience extreme volatility—more than a 20-percent swing in performance either up or down—that's known as tail risk. Though it's not supposed to happen often, it's becoming more frequent and already has happened twice, both times on the downside, since 2000. That may seem infrequent, but depending on your age and your portfolio, drops like those can inflict a mortal wound on the finances for your future plans.

If a portfolio drops by 20 percent, what's left of the investments requires a 25-percent gain to fully recover to the pre-drop balance. A 30-percent loss takes a 43-percent return, and a 40-percent loss, as some investors experienced in 2008, would require a 67-percent return to break even.

Figure 6.10 reflects the years that market anomalies—either extreme gains or extreme losses—have happened. The positive gains are reflected to the right, and though not considered normal market movement, aren't so concerning. It's the extreme losses, as shown to the left in the chart, that are worrisome. That's the tail risk and the significant market drops that we must make sure our portfolios can weather.

By limiting losses of tail-risk proportions, the recovery time from a market drop can be substantially reduced, thus increasing the longevity of assets within a portfolio.

Fig 6.10 Distribution of Yearly S&P 500 Returns

<-30%	-30 to -20%	-20 to -10%	-10 to 0%	0 to 10%	10 to 20%	20 to 30%	30 to 40%	40 to 50%	>50%
						2014			
						2012			
						2010			
						2006			
					2015	2004	2009	2013	
				2000	2011	1993	2003	1997	
				1990	2007	1988	1999	1995	
				1981	2005	1986	1998	1991	
				1977	1994	1979	1996	1989	
				1969	1992	1972	1983	1985	
				1962	1987	1971	1982	1980	
				1953	1984	1968	1976	1975	
				1946	1978	1965	1967	1955	
		2001	1940	1970	1964	1963	1950		
		1973	1939	1960	1959	1961	1945		
2008	2002	1966	1934	1956	1952	1951	1938	1958	
1937	1974	1957	1932	1948	1949	1943	1936	1935	1954
1931	1930	1941	1929	1947	1944	1942	1927	1928	1933

Tail Risk ◄——

Source: Standard & Poor's.
Data: 1927-2015.

Be Active, Not Passive

To survive the negative market anomalies and continue to thrive, an investment portfolio must have built-in protections to help it weather and minimize the losses. That eases the tail risk and helps to avoid the full effects of a precipitous market decline. At least then, a portfolio has a better chance of recovery in a time frame that's realistic for you, especially if you're a retiree.

Markets are efficient over time—long periods of time. That's time retirees and soon-to-be retirees generally don't have.

With all the doom and gloom about the ups and downs of equities markets, by now you're probably ready to run the other way or even look to your mattress as your money's best bet. But, as I've discussed, in today's low interest rate environment and with the high cost of living increasing daily, the answer isn't to run the other direction. Avoiding equities altogether is a mistake. A retirement portfolio needs the growth potential that the right equities can offer. But that portfolio also requires that an investor take the right pre-emptive and protective steps now by embracing the New ROI approach to equities management.

The Risk Factors

Adding further to the confusion and stress of investing is that more than one type of risk threatens our investing dollars.

The entire market is exposed to systematic or undiversifiable risk from external forces like interest rates, recession, and wars. Diversifying your holdings doesn't necessarily protect a portfolio from those risks. Too many investors found that out the hard way in 2008.

The other primary type of risk is unsystematic risk or diversifiable risk. It tends to be company- or sector-specific. Something could be amiss with a specific company's product, for example. Or, a product recall or labor dispute could affect a company's stock or a sector's performance. This type of risk can be minimized with true diversification of a portfolio's holdings.

Whether we like it or not, periods of systematic risk are simply a part of life. Whatever the cause, they're characterized by at least one severe market loss that's very difficult from which to recover. As you can see from Figure 6.11, since 1926, we've had at least five periods of undiversifiable risk. Those five periods averaged a 53-percent loss and led to an average of 19 years without making a dime.

Remember when I talked earlier about factor investing, a hot trend to capitalize on small-cap companies, and why it didn't work in the shorter term? That's a great example of the weakness of investing or investment trends that require extremely long time horizons to be successful. And that's why they're not a sure thing over reasonable time frames.

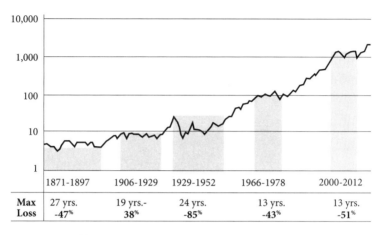

Fig 6.11 History of S&P 500 Bear Markets

Bear Markets	
Average Duration	19 yrs.
Average Max Loss	-53%

	1871-1897	1906-1929	1929-1952	1966-1978	2000-2012
Max Loss	27 yrs. **-47%**	19 yrs.- **38%**	24 yrs. **-85%**	13 yrs. **-43%**	13 yrs. **-51%**

Note: S&P 500 monthly data (1871-2015).

Understanding Beta

Oftentimes as an investor, you hear the experts talk about a stock's beta or beta coefficient. It may sound like yet another investing complexity designed to confuse people even more. Actually, a stock's beta is an easy-to-understand and important number that measures a particular stock's volatility in relation to the rest of the market. It doesn't measure the stock's standalone volatility, but rather shows how the stock stacks up against the rest of the market.

The S&P 500 Index, for example, has a beta of 1.00. It's the benchmark. A stock with a beta of greater than 1.00 is considered more volatile than the market in general as measured by the benchmark. Conversely, a stock with a beta of less than 1.0 is considered less volatile than the market in general.

For example, General Electric (NYSE: GE) has a beta of 1.20, so it's expected to move more than the market in general. That is, it's more volatile on the positive side than the general market. If the market moves upward by 10 percent, then General Electric's stock is expected to move upward by 12 percent (the mathematical equation: 1.2 x 10 = 12). Similarly, if the market drops by 10 percent, then General Electric's stock is expected to drop by 12 percent.

On the other hand, if a stock carries a beta of 0.85, then it's considered less volatile and likely to rise and fall more slowly than the benchmark and the rest of the market.

Investors leaning toward less risk may feel more comfortable with stocks that have lower betas, while those willing to accept greater risk generally opt instead for stocks with betas above the 1.00 benchmark.

Understanding Standard Deviation

Unlike beta, which compares an investment's performance to a benchmark, standard deviation is a number that stands alone as an indicator of an investment's volatility. Yes, it's yet another number, but it's also relatively simple to understand and even to figure out yourself if need be, thanks to online calculators and basic computer software like Excel.

Basically, standard deviation uses an investment's annual rate of return and measures how much that investment historically moves from its mean. A mean, of course, is the average, as in the expected normal returns for an investment.

The greater the standard deviation, the more volatile the investment. Therefore, the higher the number, the greater the volatility, or the lower the standard deviation of a stock, the less the volatility.

Last Words

Let's review some of the essentials discussed in this chapter:

- Losses have a greater impact on a portfolio than gains.
- Following a loss, what's left of a portfolio has to work that much harder to recover from the loss, without even factoring in any gains necessary to reach financial goals.
- A 50-percent loss requires a 100-percent gain simply to return to breakeven.

- Long-term successful investing is a lot about learning how not to lose.

- The timing of a loss also affects the severity of that loss. If it occurs during the few years prior to or immediately after retirement, the effects can be even more dramatic and lasting.

- Our everyday market roller-coaster—ongoing ups and downs—further complicates the ability of a portfolio to recover from a serious loss.

- The 2008–2009 market collapse cost older Americans literally trillions of dollars, and that's only counting losses to 401(k) savings and defined contribution retirement plans.

- The momentum of losses can be substantial. Since 1926, the stock market has dropped at least 10 percent 29 times. In nearly half those instances, markets had dropped by more than 20 percent before the freefall was over.

- The impact of losses is exacerbated if someone is already counting on his or her portfolio for regular living expenses or withdrawals.

- Savvy investors realize the importance of building into their portfolios protections from devastating losses—protection like that offered by the New ROI strategy for equity investing.

- Our investing dollars are exposed to two types of risk. Systematic or undiversifiable risk affects the entire market and includes external forces like interest rate swings, recessions, and wars. Unsystematic or diversifiable risk tends to be company or sector specific and can be limited somewhat by real portfolio diversification.

- A stock's beta as well as its standard deviation help explain its degree of volatility, in terms of a benchmark (beta) and compared with its historical rate of return. (standard deviation).

Now It's Your Turn

To help you take control of your investing portfolio with the New ROI in mind, some questions to ask yourself about your investing, portfolio, and financial future include:

- Do you know and understand the full and far-reaching effects that losses can have on a portfolio and on the security of your retirement financial future? Any investor today really can't afford not to pay attention.

- Do you know that a 50-percent loss requires a 100-percent gain simply to return to breakeven? The financial road to recovery is steep, and fraught with plenty of potholes and roadblocks.

- Are you aware that the timing of a loss can have a dramatic impact on the reliability of your income in retirement? A loss during the retirement risk zone—the five years before retirement and the five years after—could increase the chances that your money won't last your lifetime.

- Are you regularly withdrawing money from your nest egg for living or other expenses? If so, even small losses can add up to almost insurmountable ones and make portfolio recovery especially difficult.

- How tough is it to recover from losses? Mathematically speaking, the probabilities can be staggering.

- Have you thought about taking pre-emptive steps today to minimize potential portfolio losses? If you haven't already, you should. That's a major tenet of the New ROI equity portfolio management approach.

7 Minimizing Risk and Cutting Your Losses: Your Personal Built-In Stop-Loss Plan

NOW THAT YOU understand the impact losses can have on a portfolio, you can take the necessary actions ahead of time to make sure to keep potential losses in check if and when they occur. It's time to put in place your own personal plan to stop the losses, what the "New ROI" equity strategy refers to as stop-loss.

As you've read throughout these pages, the solution to avoiding losses clearly isn't to stay out of equities altogether. Equally implausible is the argument that if someone can't risk loss of principal, he or she shouldn't be in the stock market. Or, the argument continues, that person should at least be invested in less volatile investments like money-market funds and CDs.

But with today's rising costs of living, changing lifestyles, and longer lifespans, the individual investor simply can't afford to risk his or her financial future on outdated investing strategies. Instead, the New ROI seeks to control equity volatility and limit investment depreciation and decimation by building in stop-loss protections.

A New Breed

The New ROI stop-loss differs from typical portfolio risk management in that most portfolio managers try to manage risk and limit losses through asset allocation with periodic rebalancing. That is, they spread a portfolio's holdings across various asset classes—whether by market capitalization, different sectors, types of investments, or a combination.

To further minimize risk, the portfolio spread is then reallocated or rebalanced annually or, in some cases, more frequently. Unfortunately, that rebalancing doesn't always occur, and when it does, it often isn't enough to fully protect a portfolio today. If rebalancing is done properly—with the New ROI in mind, and either with the help of the right advisor for the most optimal performance, or on your own—it may work to help insulate a portfolio from diversifiable risk. Remember: That's risk that can be managed by allocating assets across different industries or sectors of the economy. Rebalancing in that manner, though, does not inoculate a portfolio from systematic or undiversifiable risk, as discussed in the last chapter. Those risks and their potential for losses affect the entire market and can be the result of interest rate swings, recessions, war, and other similar events.

The better, more inclusive approach to risk management, especially in our volatile times, is stop-loss. With the right advisor, one who embraces the New ROI, stop-loss becomes a mathematically precise and scientific 24/7 portfolio monitoring process to maximize gains and minimize losses. But, you, too, can gain an investing edge with a simplified do-it-yourself version of stop-loss.

Let's look more closely at how to implement your own stop-loss program to give your money the fighting chance it needs to grow and meet your financial needs now and into and throughout retirement.

The Magic Number

First, let's be clear about what stop-loss is and what it is not, and what it can and can't do.

Don't expect stop-loss, whether you do it yourself or through an experienced financial advisor, to be a cure-all. In a market freefall, it won't prevent all portfolio losses. But it will limit those losses to more manageable numbers so that your money actually has the chance to recover and grow properly within a reasonable time frame.

Remember Peter and Alice from earlier and how their nest egg was devastated by the 2008 market collapse? If they had, instead, embraced the

New ROI, the collapse would have had a negligible effect on their $500,000 portfolio and retirement plans.

Not an Everyday Occurrence

Stop-loss is not a strategy that relies on portfolio churn. An investor doesn't face the prospect of regularly selling off his or her equities in favor of safe havens, anxiously watching the markets for signs of recovery, and then at the appointed time buying everything back again, and repeating the process over and over.

Instances in which investors invoke stop-loss are rare. Over the past 22 years, market drops have triggered only five stop-loss actions. Figure 7.1 reflects those five stop outs—jargon for stopping portfolio losses by selling off the equities. It also shows when the stock buyback happened and how the New ROI equities portfolio performed compared with the S&P 500 in the interim.

For example, the first stop out happened September 1, 1998, and lasted just three months, with buyback on December 1st of that year. That stop out proved incorrect. The New ROI portfolio only earned 2.16 percent, whereas the S&P 500 earned 18.70 percent during those three months. Remember when we discussed the momentum of losses, though? A 10-percent drop in the market becomes a bear market 45 percent of the time. In other words, roughly half the time the stop out is a false alarm.

Even with misses like that, the New ROI still works because the stop-loss move halts losses and likely will rebound with at least a small gain. More important, however, is the other 50 percent of the time when the stop out is the right move—when that 10-percent market decline becomes a destructive bear market. In those instances, the stop out prevents a portfolio from hemorrhaging losses.

The stop outs of 2000 and 2008, for example, illustrate the power of the New ROI. In those cases, the drops lasted much longer, and resulted in a 23-percent loss in the first bear market and a 35-percent drop in the second. The defensive New ROI portfolio generated a positive 18 percent during the first stop out, a 41-percent improvement. That was followed by 4 percent in the second bear, a 39-percent improvement.

Fig 7.1 Preservation of Capital Is the Priority

Stop-Loss Protection Date	Buy-Back Date	Duration (Months)	New ROI Portfolio	S&P 500
9/1/98	12/1/98	3.0	2.16%	18.70%
12/1/00	6/2/03	30.0	18.67%	-23.79%
2/1/08	5/1/09	14.9	4.66%	-35.10%
7/1/10	1/3/11	6.1	1.17%	24.97%
9/1/11	2/1/12	5.0	0.68%	10.84%
	Average	**11.8**	**5.47%**	**-0.88%**

 Bear Markets

Data: Back-tested simulation January 1, 1994 through December 31, 2016.
S&P 500 data provided by Standard & Poor's.

To illustrate the power of being right only half the time, let's compare long-term portfolio returns. With the New ROI approach, a portfolio experienced a 10.40-percent annualized return for the last 20 years (ending July 31, 2016) compared with an 8.21-percent return for the S&P 500. That's a 2.21-percent difference. That may not sound significant, but over 20 years that adds up to an increase of $274,000 on a $500,000 portfolio.

10 Percent and Why

The New ROI approach targets a 10-percent drop in the S&P 500 Index as the optimal point to stop the loss—to sell off a portfolio's equity holdings and temporarily park the resulting cash in a safe haven. (I'll talk about the best safe havens a bit later in this chapter.)

That number isn't arbitrary; it's backed by scientific analysis. Remember that I talked about the momentum of losses in the last chapter and what can and does happen once the market slips by 10 percent.

With the New ROI do-it-yourself version, tracking market movements doesn't have to be about constant exasperation with and worry about the daily ups and downs of markets. Instead, on the last day of each month, you can go online to check the S&P 500 Index. The information is available on plenty of websites, including Yahoo/Finance and Google/Finance, or you can use a preferred search engine or website.

If the index is down 10 percent from its high point since you purchased the equities in your portfolio, that's the signal it's time get out—to stop the loss and sell all your stock holdings across the various sectors. Take the resulting cash from the sell-off and move it temporarily into a safe haven. If the S&P is off only 9 percent, leave your equity holdings alone, and check back again in a month. If it's off any more than 10 percent, get out. Sell off the equities.

If markets seem especially volatile during any month, or if it simply makes you feel better to check the S&P 500 number more often, that's okay, too. Sometimes investors who subscribe to the DIY New ROI prefer to check the numbers more frequently, at least in the beginning until they get comfortable with the reliability of the system.

We base that 10-percent falling-markets marker on our scientifically sound back-testing, which includes 20-year scenarios that provide an accurate and honest picture of how the strategy works across all kinds of situations. However, you are only looking at the S&P once per month, so it may be down more than our 10-percent target threshold. That's not the end of the world. The important take away is that you limited your losses from becoming truly destructive and provide your money an opportunity for quicker recovery.

Fig. 7.2 Stop-Loss Illustrated

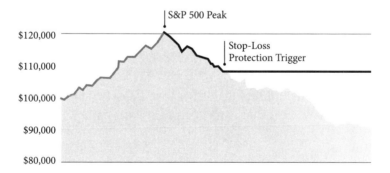

For example, the S&P 500 hit a high of 1,565.15 on October 9, 2007. Even though by March 9, 2009, the S&P had plummeted to a low of 676.53 (a 57-percent decline), with stop-loss for principal protection in place you would have targeted the sale of equities when the S&P dropped to 1,408.64 (a 10-percent decline). If you had $200,000 invested, that's a potential savings of $94,000.

This kind of pre-emptive strategy, used sparingly and adhered to even if markets improve temporarily in the interim, can be essential today to limit investment depreciation and decimation.

Temporary Parking Place for Your Cash

Of course, once you hit the 10-percent loss marker and sell your equities, what you do with the cash capital is just as important as stopping the losses. The New ROI calls for moving the cash temporarily into a stable, yet liquid, safe haven. Emphasis here, though, is on "temporary" and "stable."

I like bond ETFs—exchange-traded funds—generally from big companies that provide broad exposure to U.S. investment-grade bonds. During my years in this business, I've found ETFs from companies like Vanguard, iShares from BlackRock, and SPDR from State Street Global Advisors to be the best because they're relatively inexpensive. Invest in high-quality bonds across the spectrum—including government, corporate, and agency; the bonds offer an array of different maturities. (Incidentally, I don't work for any of these companies and get no compensation from them in exchange for suggesting their products. I simply believe these products warrant my recommendation.)

I like ETFs versus mutual funds because they're not actively managed, thus they have fewer fees that can eat away at your money.

Safe Alternatives

If you prefer other alternatives, look for a bond index fund that tracks the Bloomberg Barclays Capital Aggregate Bond Index (formerly the Barclays Capital Aggregate Bond Index; *https://index.barcap.com/ Benchmark_Indices/Aggregate/Bond_Indices*). That index represents investment grade, high-quality bonds traded in the United States.

Some possibilities include:

- Vanguard Total Bond Market Fund (Ticker: BND).
- SPDR Barclays Aggregate Bond ETF (BNDS).
- iShares Core US Aggregate Bond (AGG).

Alternatively, you can seek out other ETFs; just make sure they mirror the index.

Or, if you prefer something even more conservative than a high-quality bond fund, you can park your money temporarily in a fund that tracks U.S. Treasuries. That's the safest possible haven because it's backed by the full faith and credit of the U.S. government. Even though that doesn't quite have the same caché it used to, it's still probably the safest investment in the world.

Keep in mind, though, that—whatever the safe haven—this is a short-term arrangement because in our low interest-rate environment, you're trading returns for security. Your money left alone in these holdings longer term carries the very real risk of inflation eroding not only your principal, but eating away at any potential gains, too.

Because it's merely a short-term solution, though, the security of a safe haven is worth the tradeoff given the state of the markets in a stop-loss situation. Realistically, too, a portion of your portfolio already may be in one or both of these relatively secure holdings, depending on your risk tolerance and the breakdown of your portfolio.

All bonds, bond funds, and ETFs are not the same in terms of risk, either. The lower the credit quality of the bonds, the more returns correlate with those of stocks during bear markets. That means if markets are plummeting, so may the stability of a lower-grade bond or bond fund.

Why Bonds?

When stocks decline, investment-grade bonds are among the best diversifiers. It is extremely rare for bonds to decline while stocks are experiencing high volatility. During the 50 worst one-year performance periods for the S&P 500, bonds generated on average an 8.7-percent return.

Fig 7.3 50 Worst 1-Year Stock Returns Average

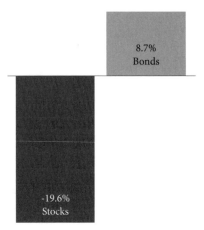

Notes: Chart illustrates the average performance during the 50 worst rolling 1-year periods for the stocks. Source: Stock returns measured by S&P 500. Bond returns measured by Barclays U.S. Aggregate Bond Index. Data provided by Standard & Poor's and Bloomberg. Data: Measured by rolling monthly from January, 1976 – September, 2016.

A bear market in bonds is much different from a bear market in stocks. A bond market is considered a bear any time bonds lose any value at all, whereas the stock market isn't considered a bear until it's lost 20 percent of its value. The worst 12-month return in bonds is barely considered a correction in stocks.

Fig 7.4 Worst Returns

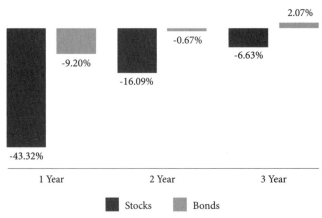

Source: Stock returns measured by S&P 500. Bond returns measured by Barclays U.S. Aggregate Bond Index. Data provided by Standard & Poor's and Bloomberg. Data: Measured by rolling monthly from January, 1976 – September, 2016.

Ignore the Detractors

Although stop-loss is a simple way to protect your money from catastrophic losses, the strategy does have its detractors.

Some people look unfavorably at the approach because it can be a favorite of day traders who continually buy and sell equities as they try to time the markets and turn profits. That's *not* what the New ROI stop-loss strategy targeting capital preservation is all about. This approach to portfolio management is utilized sparingly as an intervention to protect your principal and gains in the event of a bear or near-bear market.

Some institutions and less-than-scrupulous advisors also may try to complicate stop-loss unnecessarily to discourage its use. Or, they may be reluctant to encourage stop-loss because having your holdings in more conservative, fixed-income vehicles or held as cash cuts into their profits.

Stop-loss detractors also may claim that to beat the traditional buy-hold strategy, an investor must time his or her pullout from the market at the very top and return at the very bottom.

The New ROI stop-loss, as we've talked about, is not meant to suck every penny from the market. It's a strategy to help a portfolio grow, while at the same time protecting it from catastrophic loss.

Three-Step Process

Stop-loss the New ROI way is a three-step process and should be viewed as such to help optimize your retirement portfolio's opportunities to build for your reliability of income for the future.

The three steps are:

- Invoke stop the loss. When markets drop by 10 percent, sell off all your equities holdings.

- Temporarily transfer the resulting cash—your principal *plus* any gains—into a stable, liquid safe haven like a top-line bond fund or U.S. Treasuries.

- When markets rebound sufficiently—at the point stipulated by the New ROI, 15 percent from bottom—it's time to buy back your equity holdings.

Fig 7.5 The Stop-Loss Process: Step-By-Step

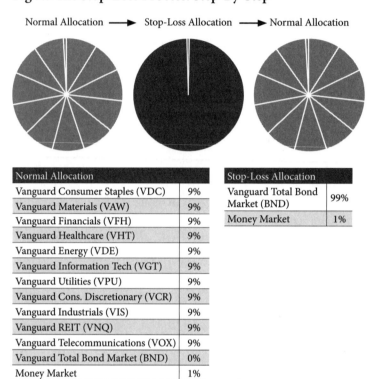

Normal Allocation ⟶ Stop-Loss Allocation ⟶ Normal Allocation

Normal Allocation	
Vanguard Consumer Staples (VDC)	9%
Vanguard Materials (VAW)	9%
Vanguard Financials (VFH)	9%
Vanguard Healthcare (VHT)	9%
Vanguard Energy (VDE)	9%
Vanguard Information Tech (VGT)	9%
Vanguard Utilities (VPU)	9%
Vanguard Cons. Discretionary (VCR)	9%
Vanguard Industrials (VIS)	9%
Vanguard REIT (VNQ)	9%
Vanguard Telecommunications (VOX)	9%
Vanguard Total Bond Market (BND)	0%
Money Market	1%

Stop-Loss Allocation	
Vanguard Total Bond Market (BND)	99%
Money Market	1%

Timing Your Buyback: The 15-Percent Mark

With the New ROI do-it-yourself strategy, a sufficient rebound is very specifically defined as an increase of 15 percent in the S&P 500 Index from the point at which the index bottomed out. Your investment dollars should remain in the safe haven until markets hit that point. The New ROI is very specific; the benchmark is not arbitrary, and it is not based on emotions or greed. It's based on mathematical research and probabilities, and scientific analysis.

As an investor, you should continue to check the S&P 500 Index once a month on the last day of the month—or more often if you're more comfortable doing so. When the S&P has rebounded 15 percent from its bottom—not the point at which you sold off your equities—it's time to get back into the stock market.

Looking for the Rebound

Once again, 15 percent is what our testing has ascertained to be the optimal number. Remember: A 10-percent loss requires an 11.1-percent gain to break even. But it can take more than that to signal a true rebound. It's important to wait until gains are greater than that minimum to avoid the whipsaws from market pullbacks that are so common today.

It's the momentum of losses I talked about earlier. Historically, when the market has dropped by at least 10 percent, in nearly half the situations the market continues downward to losses of 20 percent or more. That means, in many cases you will end up buying back your equities at lower prices than when you sold them off.

In waiting for the 15-percent rebound, you give the market the time and space to pull back and then begin its real forward momentum. If the S&P 500 is up only 14 percent, it's not the optimal time to return to the equities market. The New ROI, after all, isn't about greed, it's about gains, and holding onto and preserving those gains to meet your future needs.

Not Infallible

Stop-loss isn't always a precursor of devastating market declines. Not every 10-percent market drop turns into a bear market or signals a recession ahead. But, an investor—especially with future financial needs in retirement in mind—can't afford not to pay attention.

Setting up a stop-loss strategy for your investment portfolio is like buying insurance for your home, vehicle, or possessions. No one thinks about it or even gives it much credence until it's needed. Then it becomes a lifesaver.

The point is that investors must be prepared just in case. And, when it comes to markets, no one can truly predict how they will react or where they're going. If a stop-loss strategy in place saves an investor just once from major losses, it's well worth the minimal hassle.

If a 10-percent drop turns into a slight correction and quickly rebounds by 15 percent, an equities investor simply buys back into the market. Is it worth the effort? You bet, when you consider the power of losses and how that can annihilate a portfolio, especially because recovery in a reasonable time frame may be an impossibility.

Think about the alternative to limiting your losses, and it's a no-brainer that stop-loss matters today.

Not a New Idea

Stop-loss as a strategy isn't new. Perhaps marketers and experts figure that regularly rolling out the concept as if it were new may generate a wake-up call.

After all, so many investors get caught up in the heady gains they hear associated with investing in the stock market. As you've seen in the anecdotes that I've shared, these same people seem to willingly place their future financial security on that get-rich-quick shaky gamble that often fails to materialize.

Many of these investors overlook the fact that today's economic conditions and roller-coaster markets that often test record territory are fraught with downsides, too. Those downs come quickly and can destroy life savings with little hope of full recovery in the limited time frame most soon-to-be retirees have.

Mistakes and Misjudgments

Even though people talk about stop-loss strategies, too few investors use them on an ongoing basis to protect portfolios. Stop-loss gets used haphazardly and often isn't thought of as a pre-emptive approach to portfolio management. If you're not already prepared for and expecting stop-loss in the event of a market crash, by the time you realize it needs to be done, it's probably too late.

If someone does say he or she plans to sell off his or her equities in the event of a dropping market, or has stop-loss orders to that effect in place with his or her broker, those investors often back down on implementation when a serious market drop does occur.

Another common mistake investors make with their stop-loss strategy is that, although they may implement it in a timely manner, they jump back into the markets at the slightest uptick and ignore their pre-determined parameters of when to do so.

As a result, investors and their money can get caught up in the market whipsawing that often follows a major drop. This can negate any portfolio protections that might have resulted from the initial stop-loss action.

Re-entering the market too quickly can also have lasting and significant effects on a retirement portfolio.

For example, let's assume you (with or without a broker's or advisor's help) had in place a stop-loss plan that stipulated an equities pullout if markets drop 10 percent. Let's also assume that you chose a 10-percent market increase as the trigger to buy back into equities—rather than the 15-percent trigger that the New ROI designates. And, this happened during a sustained bear market like the one that began as a result of the tech bubble in March 2000 and lasted until October 2002. Under that hypothetical stop-loss plan, you would have sold off your equities on December 1, 2000.

With the New ROI approach and its required 15-percent index increase for buyback, investors would not have returned to the stock market until June 2, 2003. However, using the buyback-at-10-percent approach, you and your portfolio would have faced two additional equity selloffs plus two more buybacks during that same 2-and-a-half-year period. That portfolio churn combined with the whipsaw action of the markets would have resulted in a 6.6-percent decline in your portfolio's value compared with the New ROI portfolio's 18.6-percent rebound.

And, with the portfolio churn, investors with taxable dollars also could end up faced with additional tax liabilities associated with capital gains and losses.

Paying attention to scientifically proven investing fundamentals and rules does make a huge difference in the bottom line.

Stick to the Plan

One of the keys to success with the New ROI stop-loss, or of any stop-loss program, is that once the rules are set, an investor must stick with them—no questions asked, no exceptions.

This isn't about sometimes sticking to the rules or sometimes varying your strategy, depending on what's happening around you or how you feel about getting into or out of the market when you think the time is right or almost right.

The New ROI program lays out the rules ahead of time. Those rules are strict and never varied or broken. Stop-loss is the epitome of winning by not losing. This unwavering rules-based approach to investing takes into account behavioral science, and removes the emotional responses and biases from your investment decisions. It keeps your retirement portfolio on track to grow and maintain the level of gains necessary to help ensure reliability of income in retirement—over your entire retirement.

It's a strategy with growth and capital preservation in mind that's simple and efficient, and can help pre-empt potentially devastating portfolio losses.

Last Words

Let's review some of the essentials discussed in this chapter:

- The New ROI equities portfolio management strategy seeks to control volatility and limit investment depreciation and decimation by building in stop-loss protections.

- Managing risk through asset allocation and rebalancing alone isn't enough protection for your money today.

- Don't expect stop-loss to be a cure-all. It's not. But it does limit losses and prevents portfolio devastation.

- Stop-loss isn't about portfolio churn or making a fast buck. It's used sparingly—only five times in the last 22 years.

- The New ROI stop-loss trigger is a 10-percent drop in the S&P 500.

- The cash generated by any equity sell-off should be totally and temporarily parked in a true safe haven—either a stable investment-grade bond fund, similar individual bonds, or U.S. Treasuries. I prefer investment-grade ETFs.

- Continue to check the S&P 500 regularly—once a month on the last day of every month, or more frequently if you prefer. Once the market has rebounded sufficiently—defined as a 15-percent increase in the S&P 500—from the point it bottomed out, it's time to re-enter the market.

- Buy back the same allocations of the same holdings, and start again.

- Successful stop-loss strategy demands total adherence to its pre-determined rules. Sell at the appointed time, and buy back at the appointed time—no exceptions.

- Too many stop-loss strategies come up short because investors often jump back into the market too quickly after a downturn. Or they allow emotions to dictate their actions as opposed to adhering to a rules-based strategy.

Now It's Your Turn

To help you take control of your investing portfolio with the New ROI in mind, some questions to ask yourself about your investing, portfolio, and financial future include:

- Have any of your investments been caught up in the loss cycles so common in today's markets? If so, now is the time to fight back so that it doesn't happen again.

- Do you understand the importance of a stop-loss strategy to protect your retirement portfolio from the potential for catastrophic losses? It's really a no-brainer. Don't wait until after you've suffered the financial loss to wake up to the benefits of stop-loss.

- Have you thought about or tried a stop-loss strategy with an investment or your portfolio and never followed through? If so, don't be discouraged. To successfully implement a stop-loss strategy, you must get the emotion out of your investment decision-making. That means to lay down the rules and adhere to them, no matter what.

8 Real Diversification for Today's Real World: Sectors and Choices

TRADITIONAL PORTFOLIO management strategies tend to promise capital security through various iterations of asset allocation and diversification. The assumption is that diversification helps inoculate a portfolio from systematic or market risk and the potential losses associated with it.

The premise is true, but not necessarily the approach. Unfortunately, the reality is that in our increasingly interdependent and uncertain global marketplace, most of these approaches fail to really control risks and maximize gains. The result: You and your money come up short over the long term.

The "New ROI" takes portfolio growth and protection in a different direction. Rather than creating complex formulas to allocate a portfolio's assets, or buying various individual stocks and hoping they appreciate, the New ROI achieves real and true diversification with a simple, albeit nontraditional, approach: equal sector allocation across 11 sectors of the economy. That means holdings are apportioned evenly within a portfolio. If a portfolio allocates $110,000 to equities, each sector holding would total $10,000.

It's that simple, and far less complicated and far more reliable than the typical approach to optimizing a portfolio with today's risks in mind. Sectors, after all, represent unique economic entities that generally respond very differently to any given set of circumstances. That's the case no matter where or how a company derives its sales—whether domestically or internationally—or how its stock is priced.

Let's look more closely at portfolio asset allocation and why the New ROI approach to equities investing can be your best option for true diversification and solid portfolio performance.

The Typical Approach

Most portfolio strategies try to achieve the necessary diversification and security with complex formulas that rely on market timing and spreading holdings across various asset and sub-asset classes as well as styles of investing.

Asset classes include stocks, fixed-income (including bonds), cash and cash equivalents, real estate, and commodities. Styles include growth (successful companies with high potential for future growth); value (companies, the stock of which is priced low compared with company fundamentals like earnings), or some combination of both. That portfolio mix in turn often can be combined with asset sub-styles in pursuit of further alleged diversification. An investing sub-style, for example, could include emerging growth companies.

The bottom line is that in the name of diversification, a portfolio can end up a mash-up of holdings in all kinds and sizes of companies.

Stock-Picking Aside

Plenty of investors, too, think the best path to portfolio performance is picking the right individual stocks or mutual funds. Reality, though, is quite different. If you doubt that, think about some of the major stock debacles and portfolio wipeouts of the last decades, including the collapse of Enron Corp., WorldCom Inc., Lucent, Polaroid, and Lehman Brothers.

Instead of pinning all your hopes on a hot stock that may not pay off, the major determinant in terms of portfolio performance is asset allocation—how you spread the money in your portfolio across various types of investments.

In general, it really doesn't matter how an individual stock performs. Consider IBM, for example. The computer giant's stock tends to move in tandem with general movement in its sector (technology). Or, what if you're looking for the right bank stock to capitalize on potential gains if the Fed raises interest rates? It usually doesn't matter which of the big banks you choose; all bank stocks likely will go up when rates rise.

The bottom line is that you remember this rule of thumb: The sector divisions are more important than an individual company's stock.

Fig. 8.1 Determinants of Portfolio Performance

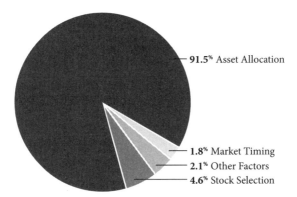

Source: "Determinants of Portfolio Performance," Financial Analysis Journal, Gary P. Brinson, L. Rendolf Hood, and Gilbert L. Beebower, 1986. "Revisiting Determinants of Portfolio Performance: An Update," Brinson, Singer, Beebower, 1991. "Determinants of Portfolio Performance III: An Update," Benson, Singer and Beebower, 1996.

More Options Still

Traditionally, investors and advisors seek to further diversify a portfolio by including equities from companies of various sizes and capitalization—large as well as small. With a goal of further diversification, investors may add companies from different industries, geographic locations, even different investing platforms.

Fig 8.2 Geographic and Value Diversification

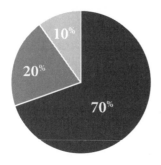

Geographic Diversification	Value
U.S. Stocks	70%
International Stocks	20%
Emg. Markets Stocks	10%

Size Diversification	Value	Growth
Large Cap	35%	35%
Mid Cap	10%	10%
Small Cap	5%	5%

Attempts at asset allocation and diversification can become even more complex as formulas call for various weightings—or percentages—of different holdings within the portfolio that vary and can change regularly.

Confusing Mix

Such portfolio mixes can be very confusing for the average investor, especially when his or her interests lie primarily in the simple goal of capturing enough potential for growth, while preserving capital and gains in the process.

The security level—or lack thereof—offered by portfolio mixes can be an issue as well. No matter how diverse-sounding a portfolio, or how many elaborate statistics or how much modeling an economist, market guru, or expert offers as proof that a strategy works, your portfolio could end up full of interdependent holdings and thus vulnerable.

Let's assume an investor or advisor decides the best approach to stability and security is a domestic-weighted portfolio, one with stocks or other holdings primarily in U.S. companies as opposed to stocks of emerging companies, foreign companies, or companies across a variety of economic sectors.

Likely stocks in that domestic portfolio could include companies like Yum! Brands, General Motors, Starbucks, and Microsoft. However, looking more closely, YUM!'s KFC brand is a huge international sensation. In 2015, GM sold more cars in China than in the United States[1], and that doesn't include the millions sold elsewhere around the world. Approximately half of Microsoft's sales are outside the United States[2], and Starbucks has announced plans to have 3,000 outlets in China by 2019.[3]

Remember, too, that even holdings that track U.S. indexes like the S&P 500, aren't necessarily "domestic" in nature. The S&P—like many diversification models—is made up of a market basket that on paper touches various commodities, industries, countries, and sectors as well as sectors within those sectors. But the reality is that the S&P isn't insulated from capital risk associated with major market swings or various sectors, especially since it often ends up weighted in favor of the hot sector of the moment.

Growth/Value and Capitalization Conundrum

Other popular methods to supposedly diversify a portfolio call for divvying up assets by growth and value investments as well as by various asset capitalization.

But research has shown that markets aren't necessarily driven by growth or value at all, and trying to diversify by buying companies of various sizes (capitalization)—a strategy known as cap-splitting—doesn't necessarily work, either, especially because no one has a crystal ball that can really predict market performance day in and day out. So, it becomes a futile and often expensive exercise to keep rebalancing, reweighting, and so on a portfolio based on already outdated parameters.

Growth/Value Debate

With our scientific tools and analysis today, we now can fine-tune market studies and actually determine what tiny segment of a supposed value or growth boom or bust actually prompted that boom or bust.

In the late 1990s, experts referred to the soaring market as a growth market. On closer examination using the latest technologies to analyze forces and movements at the time, it turns out the markets weren't powered by growth companies but instead were driven by the technology boom—the technology sector run-up.

The shift in the early 2000s to a market that earned the moniker of "value," in turn, was fueled by the boom in the energy sector. Conversely, the 2008 market collapse was blamed on a value burst. Instead, it was the bottom falling out of real estate and financial services.

Adding further confusion to the growth/value debate, companies don't always easily fall into the growth or value mold. Consider technology giants Microsoft and Intel. One would assume that both fall into the same category of growth companies because of their size and might.

Wrong. Intel is considered a growth company, whereas Microsoft is considered a value company because of, among other things, its relatively inexpensive stock that pays a good dividend—both characteristics of value companies.

Nonetheless, the growth/value debate aside, both Microsoft and Intel tend to move in tandem because they're both technology stocks. It's the sector that plays a bigger role in the stocks' movements as opposed to the value/growth dichotomy.

Heavy Weights

Capitalization-weighted approaches to equity risk management are equally flawed and do little to protect a portfolio.

That's in part because as external and internal economics shift, ongoing portfolio rebalancing is necessary to maintain the designated portfolio weighting. With that kind of active management involved, inevitably that can also allow emotion into the investing equation.

The Indexed Portfolio Fallacy

The S&P 500 is considered by many to be an excellent marker of market performance. As we briefly discussed earlier, it's a capitalization or cap-weighted index, and therefore exposes investors unnecessarily to certain bubbles.

Looking more closely, hot markets usually are led by a particular sector. In the 1990s, it was tech stocks fueling the market. In 1995, the technology sector carried a 9.4-percent weighting in the S&P. But just prior to the tech bubble collapse in 2000, technology's weighting had increased to 21.2 percent. That left even conservative investors who thought mirroring the S&P limited their risk, exposed to an aggressive sector and their money unnecessarily at risk. When the internet bubble burst, so did the retirement portfolios of unsuspecting investors.

The same sense of false security, overweighting, and subsequent catastrophic portfolio losses happened in mid-2000s with the financial and real estate sectors. That bubble burst, too, and left investors' nest eggs shattered.

Fig 8.3 Historical S&P 500 Sector Weights

	Year										
	75	80	85	90	95	00	05	10	13	14	15
Consumer Discretionaries	12.9	7.3	12.5	10.1	13	10.3	10.7	10.6	12.5	12.1	13.1
Consumer Staples	11.2	8.7	12.5	16.4	12.8	8.1	9.6	10.6	9.8	9.8	9.9
Energy	16.6	28.2	11.6	13.1	9.1	6.6	9.3	12	10.3	8.4	6.9
Financials	0.6	5	7	7.2	13.1	17.3	21.3	16.1	16.2	16.7	16.5
Healthcare	6.9	8	6.9	10.3	10.8	14.4	13.3	10.9	13	14.2	14.7
Industrials	15.2	15	14.4	11.9	12.6	10.6	11.4	10.9	10.9	10.4	10.1
Information Technology	10.7	8.7	14.8	8.8	9.4	21.2	15.3	18.8	18.6	19.7	20.4
Materials	13	9.7	7.1	7.1	6.1	2.3	3	3.7	3.5	3.2	2.8
Telecom	5.7	3.8	1.8	2	8.5	5.5	2.8	3.1	2.3	2.3	2.4
Utilities	7.2	5.6	11.4	13.1	4.5	3.8	3.3	3.3	2.9	3.2	3.1

Highest weighted sector

Source: Standard & Poor's.

As Figure 8.3 reflects, even portfolios linked to venerable index-based equities may not provide true diversification or protection. So, rather than diversification, your portfolio ends up hopelessly mired in interdependent connections that react accordingly in the event of market ups and downs. The ultimate result is you and your portfolio suffer.

The Best Option

Instead of complicated and often convoluted and misleading approaches to portfolio growth and diversification/protection, the New ROI takes a different tack. Rather than complicate portfolio diversification, which in turn complicates rebalancing and realigning and often doesn't even provide real diversification, we made it simple.

With the help of our scientific back-testing and guidance from our mathematicians and experts, we developed the chart in Chapter 5 (Figure 5.1) to help guide you to the right portfolio allocations based on your age, risk-levels, and income in retirement needs.

Simple and Clear

Rather than relying on geographically and economically intertwined equities masquerading as diversified choices, we achieve true diversification within those risk levels through equal sector allocation across the 11 sectors of the economy.

This sector division helps to maximize a portfolio's diversification, works to equalize exposure to the ups and downs of any one sector of the economy, and spreads risk broadly and equally across all the investment sectors. Those sectors are:

- Healthcare.
- Consumer discretionary.
- Consumer staples.
- Technology.
- Financials.
- Energy.
- Industrials.
- Telecommunications.
- Materials.
- Utilities.
- Real estate.

Historically, sector divisions were limited to nine or 10 sectors. The New ROI has always taken diversification a step further and included real estate as an additional sector because of its uniqueness in domestic and global marketplaces. Finally, in September 2016, Standard and Poor's recognized the important difference, too, and began to break out real estate as its own sector.[4]

Fig 8.4 Equity Allocation

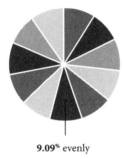

9.09% evenly

Allocation	
Healthcare	9.09%
Consumer Staples	9.09%
Consumer Discretionary	9.09%
Real Estate	9.09%
Technology	9.09%
Financials	9.09%
Energy	9.09%
Industrials	9.09%
Telecommunications	9.09%
Materials	9.09%
Utilities	9.09%

Building Blocks

These sectors are great building blocks for diversification because they are unique economic entities. Each sector in turn generally can be independent and respond very differently to a given set of circumstances. Also, a sector can rebound more quickly than an individual company's stock.

For example, when the Transocean-owned, BP-leased Deepwater Horizon oil platform exploded and sank in the Gulf of Mexico in late April 2010, the energy sector took a big hit. The accident, which killed 11 and injured many more, caused billions of dollars in environmental and economic damages—the extent of some of the damage remains unknown—and dumped millions of gallons of oil into the Gulf. By July 2010, the S&P Energy Select Sector Index had dropped more than 18 percent. It continued to see-saw, but by November of that year hit new highs.[5]

Fig. 8.5 Energy Select Sector Index TR

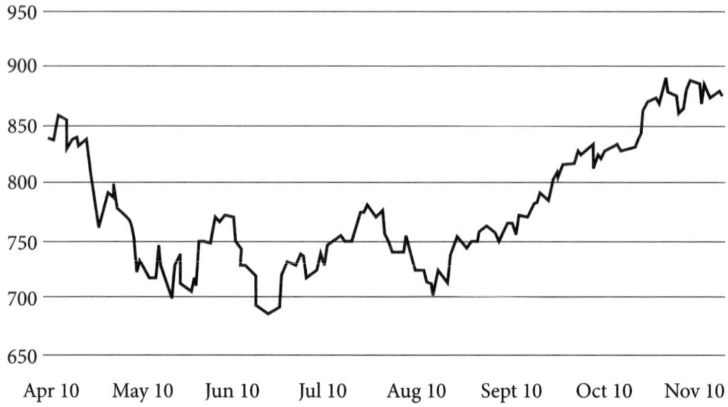

Source: www.finance.yahoo.com.

Think about it. How often do you watch or read a financial news story or hear a fund manager or economist discuss a topic without explicitly mentioning a sector of the economy? Likely not very often.

Instead, when people talk about the Affordable Care Act, or Obamacare, it's about the impact it has on healthcare companies. Or they talk about the effect of interest rates on finance companies, and so on. It's all about sectors.

Figure 8.6 offers a sample of how various sectors can react to economic scenarios—expansion and contraction—with the shaded area representing shifts in our economy. As you can see, even in an economic contraction, sectors like consumer staples, healthcare, and utilities, while to a lesser extent consumer discretionary, represent safe havens. During economic recovery, financials take the lead with industrials soaring as the economy does, too.

Fig 8.6 How Sectors React

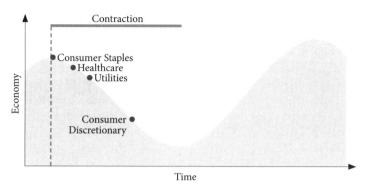

Potential Sector Catch-22

An inherent problem with typical diversification models is that, as discussed earlier, businesses and economies become interdependent as they become more global in scope. Once "diversified" assets in reality lack diversity and a portfolio becomes vulnerable. The result is that your capital is unnecessarily at risk.

An easy way to better understand this interdependence among companies and even some economic sectors is to see how they correlate—move in tandem or apart—with the S&P 500. The S&P 500 represents the benchmark.

Figure 8.7 shows the correlations of the 11 New ROI sectors. Although some sectors clearly show high correlations with the S&P 500—industrials, for example, move in the same direction as the market 92 percent of the time—others, such as utilities, real estate (as represented by REITs), energy, and consumer staples have much lower correlations and move more independently from the index. The average correlation is 76 percent.

Fig 8.7 Correlations to the S&P 500 (2000-2015)

Industrials	0.92		Growth	0.95
Consumer Discretionary	0.87		Value	0.94
Technology	0.86		International	0.87
Financials	0.85		Average	0.92
Materials	0.83			
Heathcare	0.80			
Telecommunications	0.76			
Consumer Staples	0.65			
Energy	0.65			
REITs	0.64			
Utilities	0.52			
Average	0.76			

Source: Dimensional Fund Advisors.
Data: July, 2000 – December, 2015.

Source: Beacon Capital Management, Inc.
Data: July, 2000-December, 2015.

Now compare that with the typical building blocks used for diversification: growth, value, and international asset classes. The average correlation with the S&P for all three is 92 percent. That means they move with the market 92 percent of the time—hence they offer very little diversification.

If you compare the long-term performance of various sector allocation strategies over a 20-year period ending in 2015, the 11-sector allocation approach returned 8.95 percent, the more common 10-sector allocation 8.71 percent, and the S&P 500, 8.06 percent. The 11-sector division simply adds a bit more insurance as protection for your money.

The New ROI portfolio doesn't include a global sector, but it does have international exposure because of those correlations we talked about earlier. Also, within each sector, companies themselves have domestic and global exposure because of that same interconnectivity. Ford Motor Company, GM, and Microsoft, for example, have operations and major sales worldwide.

Minimizing Losses

Markets, we all know, are reactionary in nature, so there will be upturns and downturns, gains and losses. But, with the New ROI equal sector allocation, your risk is spread equally across 11 sectors. It's not weighted toward one sector or the other. If one sector collapses—no matter if it was the hot ticket, market darling or not—your portfolio's losses are limited by stop-loss and by the limited exposure to that one collapsed sector.

In the biotech sector run-up and then subsequent collapse of 2015, for example, with the equal sector approach, your losses would have been limited to 9.09 percent—the extent of the healthcare sector's percentage allocation in your portfolio. No matter whether a sector is hot at the moment or not, equal sector allocations means a portfolio is evenly divided among the 11 pre-designated sectors: 9.09 percent of your equities are in each sector. That means 9.09-percent exposure to each sector.

And remember: Even in the event of a market-wide collapse, it's unlikely your losses would be significantly more than 10 percent—the stop-loss threshold. Once again, it's not about greed and capitalizing on every penny run-up possible. The New ROI is about enabling your nest egg to grow while protecting it and your gains over the long haul to ensure reliability of income in retirement.

Moderating Volatility

How successful is this approach? Sector returns can vary widely. Over the last 10 years, the difference between the best performing and worst performing sectors has been more than 30 percent per year. The New ROI is designed to moderate that volatility with its equal sector divisions.

Again, in that 2000 technology bubble, the S&P was highly vulnerable to a loss because of its heavy weighting toward technology. When the bubble burst, the S&P lost 9 percent in 2000 alone, primarily the result of the 36 percent drop in technology stocks. Meanwhile, a portfolio with equally weighted sector allocations—the New ROI—gained slightly.

Equal sector weighting is the New ROI's first line of defense to protect your portfolio from the natural bubbles that can and do occur in various sectors.

As you've seen throughout these pages, the New ROI is an outperform-er over time. The strategy comes out ahead year after year across market expansions and contractions, and in both the short-term and long-term.

Fig. 8.8 New ROI Portfolio vs. S&P 500

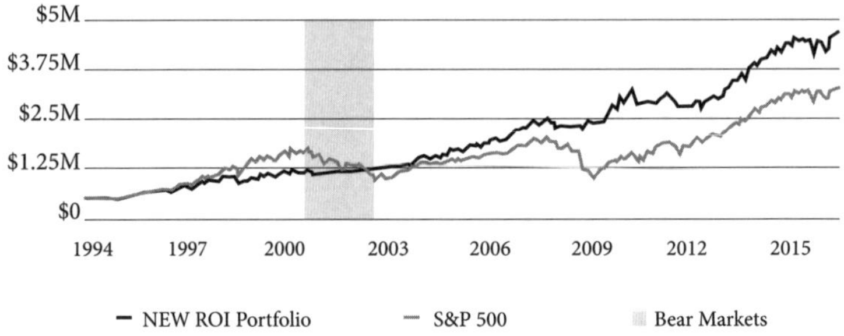

Data: Back-tested simulation January 1, 1994 – June 30, 2016.
S&P 500 data provided by Standard & Poor's.

The Value of Being Prepared

In 2007, Bill was determined to make the right moves with his retire-ment portfolio. When he heard and read that real estate was the ticket to riches with prices that had soared 150 percent in the last five years, he took the hype bait and jumped in feet first. With his advisor's blessing, he weighted his portfolio heavily in REITs (real estate investment trusts).

At first, it looked as if Bill's financial future was secure, but then real-ity set in. Remember what usually happens when someone tries to get in on the hottest, latest, and greatest? Often by the time you jump on that band-wagon, it's too late to come out a winner. Unfortunately for Bill, that's what happened, and he watched helplessly as another bubble burst, decimating his portfolio. Real estate lost 16.50 percent in 2007, and another whopping 37 percent in 2008 as the financial crisis peaked. Ultimately, Bill's "sure-thing" gamble on real estate cost him 47 percent of his portfolio's value. That meant his $500,000 portfolio had shrunk to $265,000.

Jim, age 55 in 2005, had mapped out his retirement saving strategy. If he worked 10 more years—until 2015—his $500,000 would grow enough to provide what he needed for a comfortable lifestyle in retirement. He was an avid fisherman and planned to travel to as many of the ultimate fishing spots as he could around the country and even in South America. Ultimately, Jim hoped to have saved $1 million by the time he turned 65 and retired.

Jim also astutely recognized—unlike our friend Bill—that the hottest, latest, and greatest investment craze was not the ticket to filling his retirement coffers. Too much—his future financial security—was at risk. He also knew he still needed his money to grow and that the traditional CD and Treasuries approach couldn't produce the gains he would need to fund his dream and future living expenses.

So, Jim opted to split his retirement portfolio, allocating 50 percent to funds that mirrored the S&P 500 Index—the general market—and 50 percent in a fund that mirrored the (conservative) Barclays Aggregate Bond Index. Because Jim needed 7.2-percent growth each year to reach his $1 million retirement goal by 2015, and this portfolio mix historically generated 8.7-percent growth, the allocation seemed reasonable.

Then came the collapse of 2008. Jim's seemingly conservative portfolio—even with 50 percent invested in "safe" bonds—had to absorb a 17-percent loss. Jim's portfolio didn't recover that loss until two years later. Only then, could Jim begin to rebuild his nest egg. Now, rather than coast into retirement easily in 2016, Jim faced the option of either continuing to work and wait until he reached his financial objective or drastically slash expectations for his income and lifestyle in retirement.

If Jim instead had embraced the New ROI portfolio management strategy, the 2008 market collapse would not have had such a devastating and long-lasting effect on his portfolio. Jim would have been able to easily reach his $1 million target by 2015.

Last Words

Let's review some of the essentials discussed in this chapter:

- Our increasingly interdependent, global marketplace has blurred the traditional lines of diversification when it comes to portfolio holdings. Traditional asset allocation and diversification no longer offer enough capital security.

- Stock picking, complex formulas for asset allocation, and market timing strategies don't work well today, either—nor do the typical portfolio building blocks like growth, value, and international asset classes.

- In truth, too much of the traditional portfolio allocations tightly correlate with movement of the market, negating any diversification advantage.

- Sectors tend to have less correlation with the general market, move more independently, and therefore provide better diversification.

- Rather than play into market bubbles—and therefore expose a portfolio to unnecessary risk—the New ROI subscribes to equal sector weighting as your equities portfolio's first line of defense.

- The New ROI further protects your portfolio with a stake in all eleven financial sectors.

- Over the long-term, the New ROI outperforms the general market as measured by the S&P 500.

Now It's Your Turn

To help you take control of your investing portfolio with the New ROI in mind, some questions to ask yourself about your investing, portfolio, and financial future include:

- Have you thought about the real diversity, if any, in your portfolio? Too often a retirement portfolio's holdings end up concentrated in one or more stocks or industries, and in turn leave a nest egg vulnerable and defenseless.

- How many different economic sectors are represented in your portfolio? Take another look at your holdings to determine if rather than diversified, your portfolio is dependent on one sector or even on part of one sector.

- Have you considered what could happen to your nest egg in the event of another market collapse like that of 2008? It's not a matter of if it will happen; it's when. That's simply the nature of our economy and investing today.

- Does your portfolio have built-in diversification and protection against major losses? All it takes is one major loss to devastate your financial future.

- Why not ask your advisor about or get started on your DIY 11-sector New ROI approach to portfolio diversification, protection, and management today? It's much easier to do than you may think.

Part

3 What Works for You

9 There's No Such Thing as "Fee-Free" Investing: How to Keep Fees Low

FEES CAN ADD UP, often to the point where they can hinder a portfolio's growth. After all, every dollar you pay in investment costs is a dollar that can't appreciate in your portfolio.

Robo-investing strategies—those automated services that use algorithms to manage portfolios and advertise barely there fees up-front—can also extract hefty fees elsewhere down the road.

The solution to this fee overload sounds simple: cut out the costs. The problem is it's not as easy as it sounds. Too often, many investors aren't even aware of all the costs of an investment or that a portfolio incurs.

Fees: A Hard Habit to Break

For years, people have spouted the mantra "Keep fees low." To be fair, fees—at least the advertised ones—have indeed fallen in recent years. Investors are moving toward lower-cost funds and even some less expensive approaches to investing.

Yet too many investors keep paying the high cost of investing. It's not always about no-load or low-load fees, either. Today there are plenty of ways to pay little or nothing in up-front investing costs. It's the other fees we sometimes overlook or don't know about that can exact a heavy toll on our portfolios.

Unraveling the Confusion

Generally, investments have two major types of fees: transaction and ongoing. Transaction fees are incurred when you buy, sell, or trade an investment. Ongoing fees such as annual maintenance or management are expenses incurred on a regular basis.

Again, this sounds rather straightforward, but it isn't. Often an investor isn't even aware of all the fees associated with an investment until after the fact, when those fees already have been deducted. On the other hand, some people never even realize that they've paid some of the fees. That's one more reason why it's so important to make sure you're aware of *all* the fees and expenses of any investment before you put your money down.

Bear in mind, though, not all fees are bad or necessarily unfair. However, it's important to know what you're being charged, when, and why. Before you buy an investment, make sure to ascertain the total fees involved—including those as part of the purchase, ongoing maintenance, and any sales. Then, factoring in all those fees, determine how much the investment will have to grow in order for you to break even. That can be an eye-opener.

Don't feel you're alone in not understanding all the fees or how an advisor is compensated. You're not. In fact, almost seven in 10 people are somewhat or totally confused about fees even after reading a financial statement from their broker, according to a survey commissioned by the U.S. Securities and Exchange Commission.[1]

Even investors who turn to no-load funds (a designation for mutual funds that don't charge fees up-front or at the back end when they're sold) end up paying fees. Mostly they're management fees that aren't readily visible, but they eat into portfolio gains.

A Few of the Fees

Here's a sampling of fees and expenses you could be paying—knowingly or not—in connection with an investment.

- **Annual operating expenses.** ETFs and mutual funds are managed by investment professionals who incur costs for their services that are passed on to investors as fees deducted from the fund's assets; can include management fees,

12b-1 fees, and other expenses; often referred to as a percentage of the fund's assets—the fund's expense ratio (identified in the fund's prospectus as the total annual fund operating expenses).

- **Commission.** Compensation a firm or financial professional earns acting as an agent in a securities transaction. The low-cost, discount brokerages also earn some fee—usually a flat fee—for their services.

- **Investment advisory fees.** Charged by a professional investment advisor to manage your portfolio; these fees are annual and can be fixed or based on a percentage of the portfolio's value.

- **Markdown.** When a security is sold to an investor at a price lower than market price, the difference or discount is the markdown.

- **Markup.** A broker/dealer who sells you a security from its inventory is a principal in the transaction and is compensated for that by selling the security to you at higher than market price—the markup.

- **Sales load.** A mutual fund can charge a fee similar to a commission; can be front-end, which is assessed at the time of purchase, or back-end, at time of sale.

- **Surrender charge.** Typically, assessed for early withdrawal, from an annuity, for example; often a percentage of amount withdrawn.

- **401(k) fees.** The cost of operating and administering a 401(k) plan; in addition to annual operating expense of a mutual fund, for example; passed on to plan participants.

Additional fees may be assessed, too, for account transfers, minimum balances, cash transfer, inactive accounts, and more.

Performance Not the Issue

Worse still though, higher fees do not necessarily equate with stellar performance. In fact, the average actively managed mutual fund doesn't return much—if anything—after factoring in fees and expenses. That's the conclusion of a study at the University of Maryland, which examined monthly returns of more than 2,000 open-end domestic equity mutual funds. The study found that a little more than 75 percent of funds have an alpha of zero. Alpha is a measure of an investment's performance against a benchmark. A zero alpha means the funds have managers "with some stock-picking ability," but any gains as a result of those abilities are lost to fees.[2]

In a study of the 2,202 active equity funds in existence at the start of 2001, only 476 were considered successful at year-end 2015. The parameters for success included a fund surviving through 2015 and overall outperforming its benchmark. However, 98 percent (468) of those successful funds also underperformed their benchmarks in at least four of the 15 years ended December 31, 2015, according to analysis by Vanguard.[3]

Fig 9.1 Underperformers

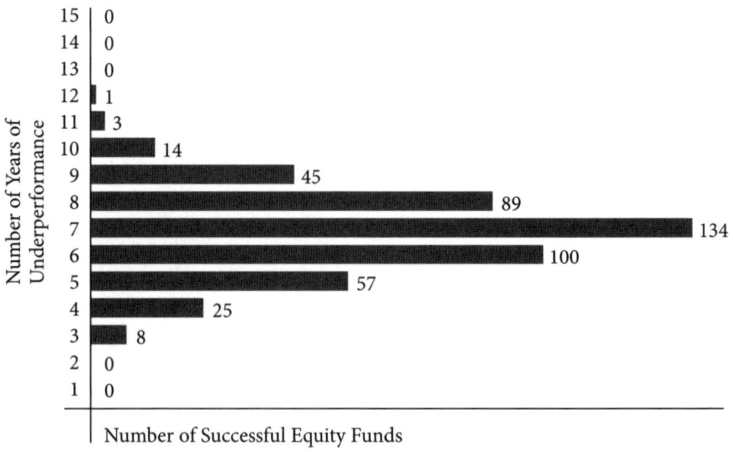

Number of Years of Underperformance (vertical axis) vs. Number of Successful Equity Funds (horizontal axis)

Years	Funds
15	0
14	0
13	0
12	1
11	3
10	14
9	45
8	89
7	134
6	100
5	57
4	25
3	8
2	0
1	0

Source: Vanguard. Data: 15 years ending December, 31, 2015.

Proof Aside

Unfortunately, despite all the numbers, and the proven higher and better long-term returns, even the most seasoned investors remain wary of and often tend to ignore less costly products or services. In fact, six in 10 investors still pay too much in investing fees, according to a study of 250,000 investors by SigFig.[4]

You already know that I like ETFs because they provide the diversification in holdings without the higher ongoing management fees of mutual funds. But they're still not fee free.

SigFig's analysis further found that investors paid on average 17 basis points for ETFs. (one basis point equals 0.01 percent; 17 basis points therefore is the equivalent of 0.17 percent of the investment's total value).

Some of the most popular ETFs are State Street's SPDR S&P 500 Trust (SPY) and Vanguard's Total Stock Market Index (VTI), which charge 0.09 percent and 0.05 percent, respectively. Yet, SigFig still found that six in 10 investors also own at least one fund with an expense ratio of 0.50 percent or higher.[5]

A Better Idea? Not Really

Despite warnings to the contrary, many investors think the best approach to building a portfolio, and a way to save on management fees, is to buy individual stocks. You'll incur transaction fees, but then can avoid the ongoing management fees. That may sound like a solid cost-saving approach. The problem, however, is that in exchange for less ongoing costs, a portfolio can instead face a dramatic increase in risk exposure.

With a sector's total allocation in one single company stock, your money unnecessarily is left vulnerable to market volatilities. Even if you opt to spread your risk across all 11 sectors of the economy by purchasing one stock in each sector's performance leader (or even stock in several different individual companies) that still doesn't provide your money the protection it needs against market or sector volatility.

For those who still doubt that, keep in mind what can happen even to companies that once were leaders in their respective sectors. Think of Enron (energy), WorldCom (telecommunications), and Lehman Brothers (finance). All three companies were once models of success in their individual sectors. Each, for various reasons, would fall, and their stocks would fall with them. Huge numbers of retirement portfolios suffered (unnecessarily) the dire consequences of those collapses.

The Rise of Online Trading

Many investors today have moved to online trading through various discount traders and brokerage websites to save on investing and its fees and costs. A multitude of organizations offer low-cost trading. But, keep in mind, buyer beware; shop around and pay attention to pricing and services. Both vary dramatically.

Variations in Cost

Personal finance website ValuePenguin compared the base fees to trade a stock or ETF as charged by 15 online brokerages:

- Sharebuilder (now CapitalOne Investing, *www.capitaloneinvesting.com/a/main*).
- Firstrade (*www.firstrade.com/content/en-us/welcome*).
- OptionsHouse (*www.optionshouse.com*).
- Merrill Edge (*www.merrilledge.com*).
- TD Ameritrade (*www.tdameritrade.com/home.page*).
- SogoTrade (*https://sogotrade.com*).
- e*Trade (*https://us.etrade.com/home*).
- Charles Schwab (*www.schwab.com*).
- Scottrade (*www.scottrade.com*).
- Fidelity (*www.fidelity.com*).
- Tradestation (*www.tradestation.com*).
- TIAA-CREF (now TIAA, *www.tiaa.org/public/index.html*).
- Wells Trade (*www.wellsfargo.com/investing/wellstrade-online-brokerage*).
- TradeKing (*www.tradeking.com*).
- T. Rowe Price (*www3.troweprice.com/usis/personal-investing/home.html*).

Based on its research, the average cost per trade was $8.90, with the highest of $19.95 charged by T. Rowe Price, and lowest at $4.95 for both TradeKing and OptionsHouse. Broker-assisted fees were much higher: the average at $30.99, with the highest at $55 from TIAA-CREF, and the lowest $19.95 from Sharebuilder and Firstrade.[6]

Some of these and other online brokerages often offer volume and other trading discounts, so be sure to thoroughly check out what's available before using a particular service. If you don't see any special discounts offered by a service on its website, take the time to find out more.

Shop Around

Also check the website for how you can contact the company—a live chat or at least the means to ask a trading question for no charge. If a site at the very least doesn't provide the ability to easily contact them with a question, do you really want to give them your money and count on them for your portfolio's future?

ValuePenguin's research also found more charges to consider. Though not charged by all the online brokerages, some other potential fees include account maintenance or inactivity fees, minimum balance fees, minimum cash requirements to open accounts, account transfer fees, paper statement fees, and checking account annual fees.

Fig. 9.2 Costs of Online Trading

Type of Fee	Average
Per Trade	$8.90
Broker-assisted	$30.99
Account maintenance	$32.50

Source: https://www.valuepenguin.com/average-cost-online-brokerage-trading/Average Cost of Online Trading

The Difference Fees Can Make

Let's look at the actual dollars and cents of what fees mean to a portfolio over the long term.

First, it's important to note that fees have fallen dramatically over the last two decades. The Investment Company Institute (ICI), a global association of the regulated funds industry, reports that expense ratios for equity, hybrid, and bond mutual funds dropped in 2015 to their lowest level in 20 years.[7]

A fund's expense ratio is the fund's total annual expenses expressed as a percentage of its net assets. For example, a 1 percent expense ratio translates to $10 for every $1,000 invested. A $10,000 investment, therefore would carry a $100 per year expense.

In 2015, the average equity fund expense ratio was 68 basis points, or 0.68 percent. For bond funds, it was 54 basis points or 0.54 percent, according to ICI tabulations. Just 15 years ago, those numbers were 0.99 percent for equity funds and 0.76 for bonds.[8]

Fees Add Up

That may sound like very little difference, but fees can quickly add up. Mike and Liz started off with $10,000 each in their retirement portfolios. Liz, who always did her homework before making a big financial commitment, found a low-cost ETF with annual expenses of 0.5 percent. Mike, on the other hand, figured all mutual funds were pretty much alike in terms of expenses (we all know how wrong that is!), and he ended up with a fund that charged 1.5 percent annually in fees.

Both portfolios earned a comfortable 10-percent annual return before expenses.

After 20 years, Mike's nest egg had grown to $50,000, while Liz's original $10,000 had climbed to $60,000. That's a big difference and demonstrates that fees definitely have an impact on a portfolio, especially over the longer term.

Starting Small or Big: A Case Study

Whether a portfolio starts out big or small, the impact of unnecessary high fees hits home. The following example shows the added value lower fees can bring to a portfolio that starts out with a much bigger chunk of cash.

Even though others cautioned Rachel and Sean about paying overly high fees on their investments, the couple and their financial advisor (not an advocate of the "New ROI" approach) decided on one mutual fund as the best option for their retirement financial future. So, in 2000 they invested all their $100,000 401(k) plan in that actively managed fund. Remember: An actively managed fund generates higher—often significantly higher—costs of ownership. The fund's fees included a management fee of 0.25 percent and a 0.25 percent 12b-1 fee to be paid for distribution, which added up to a total 0.50 percent in annual fees.

Meanwhile, their best friends, Sam and Cindy, roughly their same age, opted instead to take the more passive New ROI approach to equities in their retirement portfolio. With the help of their advisor, who had actually introduced them to the potential benefits of the New ROI, the couple opted to invest $100,000 in ETFs. By investing in lower-cost ETFs, they saved on fees. Their costs amounted to 0.25 percent per year.

Fast-forward 15 years and assume that both portfolios earn 8 percent every year. That's hypothetical, though, since we know the up-and-down nature of markets. A portfolio can average 8 percent, but that includes good years and bad. Let's make the assumption anyway, to help us isolate and simplify the effects fees can have on a portfolio.

After 15 years, Rachel and Sean's portfolio had grown to $295,888, and Sam and Cindy's nest egg topped $316,776. That "slight" difference in investment fees cost Sam and Cindy nearly $21,000. To make matters worse, the difference in fees becomes larger as a portfolio grows because, as I've discussed, those ongoing fees often are based on a percent of the portfolio's assets.

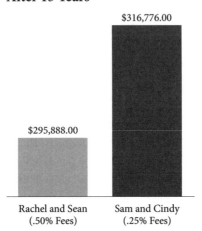

**Fig 9.3 Portfolio Values
After 15 Years**

$316,776.00

$295,888.00

Rachel and Sean   Sam and Cindy
(.50% Fees)   (.25% Fees)

Before You Think High Costs Are Passé...

Many investors, including Sam and Cindy and Liz, are opting for low-cost funds as load-based and fee-heavy funds lose their luster. Industry studies support that finding. In fact, over the last decade, 95 percent of investing cash flows have been into funds in the lowest-quintile for expenses, according to research by Morningstar.[9]

Further, 63 percent of mutual fund share classes and exchange-traded products have cut their expense ratios, and investors have noticed. Mutual funds and exchange-traded products, like ETFs with expense ratios ranking in the least-expensive quintile of all funds, attracted an aggregate $3.03 trillion of estimated net inflows during the past 10 years, compared with only $160 billion for funds in the remaining four quintiles.

But before we write the obituary for high fees, consider that only about 24 percent of fund share classes dropped fees by more than 10 percent. And 21 percent actually boosted their fees, Morningstar reports.

More on How Much Investors Can Lose

Still not thoroughly persuaded it's time to ditch those high-fee investments in favor of less-expensive ones? That's even if, by opting for a low-cost mutual fund or ETF with lower fees, you and your portfolio can come out ahead?

Lower fees and investing costs absolutely translate into more cash in hand over the long term, especially when it comes to reliability of income in your retirement.

Let's look at another example, this time involving an employee's 401(k) plan investment. It's essential to pay attention to fees within an employer-sponsored retirement plan. They can cut into a portfolio's bottom line as much as with a self-directed retirement portfolio.

Paul started saving for his retirement in 1985 with a 401(k) account through his employer with $25,000. (Of note: Paul began saving at a time when there weren't the same limitations on similar account savings as we have today.) He knew he wasn't a very good saver, but figured he had plenty of time. He also decided that if he put enough money into the right invest-ment, it potentially could grow enough to serve his needs if he made it to retirement at the end of 2015. That's not necessarily a good idea for retire-ment saving with reliability of future income in mind, but it's another good illustration of the impact fees can have.

Over the next 30 years, Paul never added a dime to the initial invest-ment. Over that time, his account averaged a 7-percent return. Luckily, in 1985 his original employer had chosen a plan with relatively low fees: 0.5 percent. By the time Paul retired at the end of 2015, his nest egg had grown to $165,000.

In contrast, though, what if the fees and expenses for Paul's 401(k) weren't as reasonable? Many aren't, even today. Let's assume the fees for Paul's investment had instead amounted to 1.5 percent annually. If that had been the case, Paul would have ended up with only $125,000 after 30 years. That 1-percent difference in fees would have reduced his 401(k) balance by 24 percent.

If you're fortunate enough to work for a company that still offers a built-in retirement plan, don't always assume it's the best retirement sav-ings alternative, or that the employer automatically has chosen a plan ad-ministrator that's cost-effective for you. The low-cost kid on the block or the top performer isn't always the option an employer selects. As with any other investment, ask questions and find out the total costs involved. Then, do your homework to determine if the costs are worth the potential for gains.

With help from the SEC's Office of Investor Education and Advocacy, Figure 9.4 illustrates just how much difference lower expenses can make.

Fig. 9.4 Portfolio Values Over 30 Years

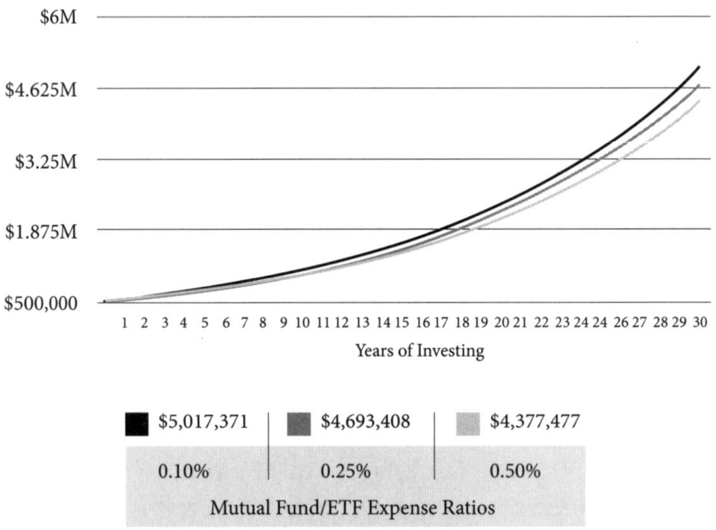

Years of Investing

	$5,017,371		$4,693,408		$4,377,477
	0.10%		0.25%		0.50%

Mutual Fund/ETF Expense Ratios

Notes: Illustrating 8% annual return less mutual fund/ETF expenses.

As discussed earlier, it's not only annual fees that hurt a portfolio's growth. As examples in this chapter have clearly shown, ongoing expenses also can cut into nest eggs over time. As with losses, the dollar amount of the fee itself is not the only loss; earnings also are lost due to the reduction in your investment balance. Over time, seemingly small fees add up, and can crush portfolio earnings.

See for Yourself

If you're working with the right advisor and are interested in learning just how much a mutual fund's or ETF's fees and expenses will cost you and your portfolio, he or she easily can provide you the information plus break down how a particular investment can affect your specific portfolio over time. That kind of personal service simply is a part of his or her job.

Or, if you prefer to go it alone, you can check out the online interactive calculator from FINRA, the Financial Industry Regulatory Authority (*http://apps.finra.org/fundanalyzer/1/fa.aspx*). Its free Fund Analyzer has information and analysis on more than 18,000 mutual funds, exchange traded funds (ETFs), and exchange traded notes (ETNs).

The ETF Advantage

As Sam and Cindy discovered, ETFs, with their lower fees, enhance a portfolio's growth potential and your nest egg's bottom line. Let's look more closely at some of the reasons why I prefer ETFs as the best investments for your New ROI portfolio.

Liquidity

ETFs most often track an index, a commodity, bonds, asset class, or sector. Unlike mutual funds, ETFs are more liquid because they're traded like an ordinary equity with intra-day price fluctuations.

ETFs generally can offer tax advantages, too, over mutual funds, because with the purchase of a mutual fund, investors also inherit the cost basis of that fund. For example, a mutual fund is required by law to distribute capital gains to shareholders if the fund's holdings are sold for a profit. That's the case even if the shareholder did not get the benefit of the full gain.

Plus, holdings within an ETF aren't usually as actively traded as mutual funds, also cutting down on expenses and fees. That means less taxes to be paid and more cash available either to add to your portfolio or use for living expenses.

Costs

The costs associated with ETFs generally are transaction fees—the cost of the initial purchase plus any commissions to the sellers.

Ongoing expenses are part of the deal, too. That can include annual operating expenses, known as the expense ratio—things like 12b-1 fees (cost of distribution and marketing of shares), and various administrative fees and costs.

To figure the annual expense ratio, a fund divides the cost of its operating expenses by the average dollar value of its assets under management.

These fees directly reduce investor returns. That's another reason to consider lower-cost ETFs.

Tracking Down the Fees

To help you get to the fee bottom line, start by reading the documents and webpages related to a specific investment—including the prospectus, online or off—as well as the brokerage or online trading organization.

Too often, investors simply don't take the time. It can be a hassle to read all that fine print, but as you've read in this chapter, it definitely pays to make the time and pay attention to every word. That's likely where you'll find many of the details related to an investment and the real financial costs associated with it.

Some Considerations

Some issues and questions to consider when assessing the actual costs of a potential investment include:

- Is there a complete list of fees and costs associated with an investment and/or an investing account? There should be, and it should include costs to purchase and maintain that investment and an account.

- Is a minimum account balance required? If so, what's the penalty for dropping below that minimum?

- What are the fees to buy, hold, and sell the investment?

- Where and how will those costs appear on an investor's account statement?

- Does an investment or provider offer any special pricing, discounts, or cost savings for specific types or amounts of trading? A group or multi-trade discount, for example?

- Does the company charge additional fees for investments held in IRAs, trust accounts, or other special accounts?

The Cost of Special Accounts

Don't overlook asking an investment company or broker about special accounts and any fees that might be associated with them. Investors, unknowingly often end up paying higher fees for special accounts.

Sometimes companies—even a discount or online broker—will offer a low transaction fee but end up charging additional for a special account like a trust or retirement account. Those extra fees more than negate any up-front cost advantages you may have realized. A company could, for example, charge an investor additional for an IRA account—perhaps an extra $25 or $50 annually.

If a company does charge extra for that special account, ask if it will waive the fees. Often, they will. If they won't waive the fee, you may want to consider taking your business elsewhere.

Also, even if they're not advertised, be sure to ask about trading or account discounts. Online and otherwise, trading organizations often offer certain discounts for larger or multiple accounts. But you have to ask.

When figuring out the most cost-effective investment and trading partner for your needs, it's important to take all the fees and services into consideration. It's about the entire package, not one single fee or lack thereof.

Last Words

Let's review some of the essentials discussed in this chapter:

- Investing and investment fees can add up. Even what start out as seemingly small amounts can, over time, seriously erode a portfolio's profits.

- Despite what you may hear about low fees, not all investments or companies adhere to the low-cost mantra.

- Read the fine print in prospectuses, in company brochures, and online. Those low or "no" fees aren't always that if you consider *all* the costs involved with buying, selling, or holding a particular investment. That includes buy and sell costs, expense ratios, annual maintenance fees, and more.

- If all the fees aren't clear to you or you don't understand any aspect of a charge to you or your account, don't be afraid to ask questions. It's your right as an investor.

- Even if a company touts its no-load funds, find out how much that investment will cost you. Nothing is free.

- Tax liabilities associated with a particular type of investment should be taken into consideration when determining total costs.

- Not all online trading organizations are created equal—either in terms of trading costs or ongoing fees.

- Consider ETFs as an alternative to traditional favorites like mutual funds, even low-cost ones. ETFs can save on ongoing management fees and taxes since they're not as actively managed or traded.

- Don't automatically assume a company's 401(k) plan or even its defined benefit retirement plan is the low-cost provider. Sometimes you may be able to opt for a lower-cost alternative.

Now It's Your Turn

To help you take control of your investing portfolio with the New ROI in mind, some questions to ask yourself about your investing, portfolio, and financial future include:

- Do you know how much you're paying for any or all the investments in your portfolio? Have you ever added them up? You should, because often you're paying too much.

- What is the actual annual cost of that no-load or low-load mutual fund you own? What about that inexpensive approach—robo-investing or that discount online broker, for example? Don't assume that just because an investment or an approach to investing is free or inexpensive upfront, that you're actually saving money in the long run. It can be the opposite.

- Do you have a 401(k) plan or defined benefit plan through an employer or former employer? If so, check to make sure you're paying the least possible for the service. Sometimes, you're not.

- Are any fee or cost discounts available for an individual investment or trading account if, for example, you maintain a certain dollar amount in your account or purchase or maintain a certain volume of an investment? Even if a company doesn't advertise those kinds of discounts, they're often available if you ask.

10 Your Options: Find an Advisor or DIY?

NOW THAT YOU have the tools to use the "New ROI" strategy to your advantage and grow your portfolio, it's time to decide whether to hire an advisor to help you or do it yourself.

Which route you take is a personal choice. There's no right or wrong answer. The important choice, however, is the make sure the New ROI strategy is in place.

Let's look more closely at the various options.

Do-It-Yourself (DIY) Approach

Given the choice, we all like to save money. In addition, the possibility of calling our own shots and making our own investment decisions may sound particularly enticing to some people. Adding to the enticements, we're bombarded constantly by slick television, internet, and radio ads touting DIY everything—investing included—as the powerful ticket to success. Online discount brokerages constantly peddle low-cost stock trades and advice, too.

Small wonder many people begin to think the only option for investing success is DIY.

With a DIY approach, you are your own boss. You make the decisions. The buck stops with you, literally.

No Deviations

If you opt for that approach, the New ROI strategy must be set in stone—no deviations. That means if one day you get what you think is a great stock tip, ignore it! An essential part of the success of the New ROI approach is to stick with it, with no variation.

Opting for the New ROI do-it-yourself approach and then only partially committing to its pre-set rules—when, what, and how to buy; when and how to sit it out; and when, what, and how to sell—undercuts your opportunities for greater portfolio growth and stability. It also can severely curtail your achievement of the new ROI—reliability of income in retirement.

In fact, failing to stick to the New ROI rules completely—allowing emotions like fear and greed into your investing decision-making and jumping into and out of markets at the wrong time—can potentially exact a huge financial toll on a portfolio.

Wired for DIY?

The bottom line is that not everyone can accept, let alone excel at, DIY investing of any kind.

In more than two decades with my firm, Beacon Capital Management, I've seen many investors try it on their own. Some succeed; others don't. I've also encountered many people who tried DIY and failed to recognize their investing mistakes until it was almost too late.

If you choose DIY investing, it can be helpful to occasionally work with a financial advisor as a partner. That partner can help you initially figure out and build your retirement portfolio, and also periodically be someone to turn to for advice and guidance. It can be a win-win; you still call the shots, but you also have the advantage of occasional advice from a trained professional.

Take Control of Your Financial Future

Whether you opt for DIY, hire an investor, or a combination of both, a big part of the decision is taking control of your financial future.

As we've discussed, to avoid becoming a financial victim you must learn to tune out the investing chatter and make the right moves now and in the future with the New ROI in mind. In doing that, you'll enhance your money's ability to provide a reliable stream of income in retirement.

Be Honest in Your Assessments

It's time to ask yourself important questions, and be honest in your answers. Your financial security is at risk.

Are you wired for DIY investing? Are you comfortable with doing it all yourself—making the necessary decisions and adhering to a pre-set, rules-based approach to portfolio management, no matter what? Can you keep your emotions from derailing your plans when the market starts to slide or when it's edging its way back? Can you be satisfied with better returns on your investments even though you may leave some returns on the table?

These are very real and important questions that you need to answer before deciding whether to set out on a self-guided investment path, to seek out the best advisor as a partner, or to work with an advisor to manage and direct your portfolio.

No Emotion

To build a retirement portfolio with future reliability of income in mind, you simply must get the emotion out of your investing. I keep emphasizing that, but I have seen too many investors lose their savings by allowing their emotions to rule their financial decisions.

The numbers are worth repeating. The average individual equity mutual fund investor—*without* the New ROI— earned only 3.66 percent for the 30 years ending December 31, 2015. That self-directed approach compares with a 10.35 percent return for the passive S&P 500 Index.[1]

Emotions are an investor's nightmare. If at the beginning of that 30-year period, you had $10,000 to invest, you would have financially fared better by forgetting about do-it-yourself market timing, ignoring the prognosticators with their latest deal of the moment, and simply putting your money in a fund that mirrored the S&P 500. You would have more than doubled your portfolio's performance over that same time just by ignoring the do-it-yourself route.

The bottom line for the DIY investing approach: Can you be mechanical in your financial philosophy and completely stick to the New ROI strategy? If the answer is yes, then DIY can be a great approach.

If the answer to either part of the question is no, then you may want to look at an alternative approach—turning to a professional financial advisor.

The Financial Advisor Approach

Hiring a professional to help with your retirement planning and portfolio management will incur additional costs. But it also can mean additional portfolio strength.

Services Net Results

Good advice from the right professional advisor is not free. We all understand that. But keep in mind that no matter what you hear to the contrary, when it comes to advisors, free or lowest-cost isn't the best alternative. And neither is necessarily the highest-price investment advice.

It's also important to think of the cost of an advisor in the context of total return. It's similar to total return investing we touched on earlier. Whether a stock price is up or down isn't enough. With an investment, you must consider everything that is involved, including factors like interest, dividends, distributions, capital gains, taxes, and fees. An advisor brings not only a greater breadth of investment and investing experience and options, but also broader knowledge, information, access, and alternatives. All of that added valuable guidance and direction figures into the equation.

Advisors can be compensated in several ways. Some may charge flat or hourly fees for services. Other forms of compensation include commissions on securities bought and sold; a markup on certain investment products when you purchase them; a mark-down of products when they're sold, and fee- or load-based depending on the amount invested. Advisors' fees also can be based on a percentage of a portfolio's holdings.

Personal Comfort Levels

An advisor's fees, however, don't have to eat up all of a portfolio's gains. And they won't if you choose the right advisor. Just as it's important to find the right portfolio risk level, it's important to find an advisor in the right price range. You need to be comfortable with the costs associated with an advisor and with the returns on your portfolio—fees included.

Whoever you choose as your advisor also should recognize the importance of the New ROI, offer sound advice tailored to your individual risk tolerance and investment needs, work hard to hold fees as low as possible, and make sure safeguards are built in to protect your portfolio from losses.

He or she should be willing to take the time to get to know and understand you and your relationship with your money, as well as be experienced with retirement and distribution issues.

Retirement and Distribution Issues

Retirement, retirement investing, and portfolio distribution require special expertise. For example, after years of saving, there are a host of issues that need to be addressed to ensure a smooth transition from employee to retiree. Two critical and often-overlooked decisions include the best way—tax-advantageous and earnings-wise—to take payouts from pension plans and from which accounts to withdraw funds first.

Although 401(k) plans have become more common than traditional pensions, your company may still offer an old-style pension. Many clients don't realize there are options about how their monthly pension benefit will be calculated. A professional can examine your plan options and help you select the distribution method that works best for you and your family.

The other decision many clients fail to make is from which accounts to withdraw money first. As a general rule, if you are under age 70½, it makes sense to withdraw money from taxable accounts first. This allows you to continue to defer taxes on growth earned in your IRAs. But again, there are many combinations of accounts and situations. A professional can calculate how and when to make withdrawals to maximize your income.

More issues include the nuances of other retirement-related tax rules, trusts, beneficiary designations, and much more.

Too many retirees end up with advisors not well-versed in those issues and who consequently make mistakes that cost portfolios dearly. A retiree may withdraw funds from the wrong accounts at the wrong time and incur unnecessary tax liabilities.

Taxing Concerns

Another advantage of working with an advisor with the right experience involves inheritance planning. Holding certain assets or investments in various types of trusts can be easier or more advantageous tax-wise to heirs. An estate planner can help you figure out what's best for your own circumstances.

Another common, costly mistake involves retirees overlooking or missing entirely IRS-mandated deadlines. At age 70½, for example, an individual must begin withdrawing funds from certain qualified retirement accounts. The amount of that withdrawal—known as the required minimum distribution (RMD)—is calculated for each year by dividing the IRA account balance as of December 31st of the prior year by the applicable distribution period or life expectancy.[2]

These are all areas in which the right qualified advisor can provide valuable input into your retirement planning.

Missing the deadline can result in big tax penalties that can be tough for someone on a fixed income. It sounds like one of those no-brainers, but it's surprising the number of people who miss the deadline.

That's yet one more way unnecessary retirement portfolio costs can eat into the reliability of income for a retiree over the long term. And it's one more reason why it's important to work with the right investment advisor who can help provide guidance, advice, and ongoing expertise to your personal investment situation.

When Elaine first came to me as a client early in 2016, she was age 72. Up until then, she had figured she had her retirement financials well under control on her own. Unfortunately, she found out the hard way that she didn't.

It turned out that Elaine had never taken a required minimum distribution from her $1 million plus IRA. Remember: By law, she should have started withdrawing a specific percentage from that account each year beginning at age 70½.

That meant Elaine, whose retirement account totaled $1,100,632 at the end of 2015, had missed withdrawals in 2014 and 2015. She should have withdrawn $36,497 in 2014 and $40,907 in 2015. I helped her understand that she also needed to take out another $42,994 in 2016. So, to make up for the missed RMDs, Elaine had to withdraw at total $120,398 in 2016 ($36,497 + $40,907 + $42,994).

The extra withdrawals aren't the problem, however. What really hurt Elaine's nest egg were the big IRS penalties for her failure to withdraw the required funds from the IRA. Those penalties amounted to 50 percent of the missed required minimum distribution. That meant Elaine owed the IRS $38,702 in penalties—50 percent of $36,497 and 50 percent of $40,907.

The New ROI Advisor Advantage

After many years in this business managing billions of dollars in investors' money, I understand the value that the right guidance and portfolio monitoring can bring to your retirement nest egg.

Although I generally use online discounters for trades, as an investment advisor and money manager, I'm biased in favor of an approach that calls for helping people identify the right professional investment advisor to offer advice, direction, and portfolio monitoring.

That doesn't mean a DIY approach with the New ROI doesn't work. It does, and, as the numbers reflect, results in solid returns with capital protections and with the all-important result of reliability of income in retirement. This do-it-yourself New ROI approach is a very simplified version of our Beacon Capital Management more comprehensive, optimized portfolio management strategy.

DIY doesn't totally maximize your equities' opportunities for growth or completely optimize protection levels, but it definitely helps. And, it can lead to significantly better financial outcomes than traditional retirement investing strategies.

Its success, however, depends on investor discipline, and, as noted, that's a discipline many people simply don't have, or an approach others aren't interested in taking. If you're someone who does want DIY, that's great. Let's get started right now with the help of the New ROI on your road to reliability of income in retirement.

How to Identify the Best Advisor for You

As you can see, choosing an advisor is very personal. After all, major decisions that can help determine your financial future and that of your loved ones end up in his or her hands. That's why it's very important to do your homework, shop around, and ask plenty of questions before ever beginning to work with an advisor.

A good starting point in your quest to find your right advisor is to ask friends and family for referrals. Do they have an advisor they like and would recommend? Has that advisor helped grow their portfolio? Has that portfolio been protected from today's volatile investing climate?

Other sources of names for a potential advisor could be your bank or financial institution, or another financial professional. You can also check out online advisor data bases from websites such as FINRA (*www.finra.org*) or the Securities and Exchange Commission (*www.adviserinfo.sec.gov*).

Fig. 10.1 How Do Investors Find Advisors?

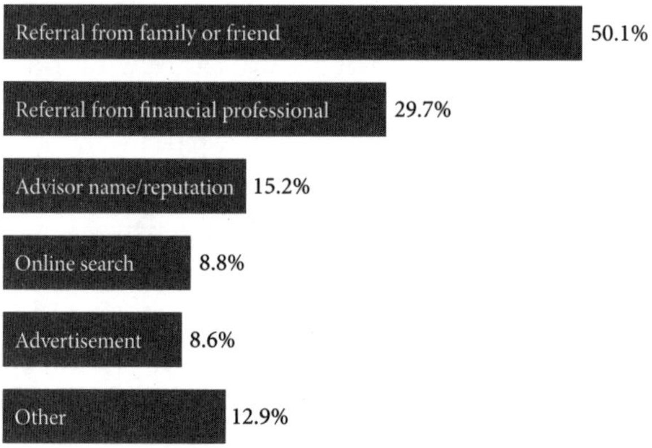

Referral from family or friend	50.1%
Referral from financial professional	29.7%
Advisor name/reputation	15.2%
Online search	8.8%
Advertisement	8.6%
Other	12.9%

Note: Figures do not add to 100% due to multiple responses. Source: Siegal & Gale LLC, "Investor Research Report" for the SEC, July 26, 2012, p. 72; https://www.sec.gov/news/studies/2012/917-financial-literacy-study-part3.pdf.

Check out FINRA's free online BrokerCheck (h*ttp://brokercheck.finra.org*), too, to help find out more about potential advisors, brokers, and brokerage firms. You can search by name, firm, and even zip code. Simply type in the name, and hit "Enter." You'll get not only a prospective broker's employment history, certifications, and licenses, but any complaints or regulatory actions against that individual as well. It's simple and takes only a few seconds. There's no point in not doing it.

Keep in mind, too, that any recommendations you receive or websites that offer information are only a first step in your advisor search. They're merely a starting point—suggestions of individuals you may or may not want to contact and follow up with for more information.

New ROI Approach

Any advisor you consider should be willing to embrace the New ROI approach to retirement planning.

Whether someone calls it that or not, he or she should understand the importance of getting the emotion out of investment decision-making. That doesn't mean you want someone who relies on robo-investing—computer-generated algorithms that dictate the "right" investments for you, when to buy, when to sell, and seldom deviate.

Nor do you want someone who pushes his or her personal "favorites"—those investments that he or she sees as the hot tickets to riches. You're not out to squeeze every penny from the market; you want growth coupled with capital security.

If the advisor is unwilling to accommodate those requests, perhaps you should consider looking elsewhere.

More on Fees

How an investment advisor is compensated for his or her time, efforts, and expertise should not necessarily determine whether you hire that advisor or not.

Despite all the opinions you read and hear to the contrary, not all fee-only advisors are good at their jobs or automatically the best choice. Free advice, too, as mentioned previously, is not necessarily the best (or the worst) advice.

Advisors who are compensated based on a percent of a portfolio's holdings have extra incentive to help grow your nest egg. It's the "more-skin-in-the game" scenario. In fact, that's one compensation method we use at my firm, Beacon Capital Management.

Any potential advisor should be evaluated individually, with compensation being only one part of the package.

Credentials and Licensing

Make sure, too, that any potential advisor has the education, training, and licensing or registration necessary to provide the services you need. You can easily find that out on FINRA's BrokerCheck.

Pay attention to the fact that just because someone claims to be licensed or registered, has a fancy website, or appears in the media as an "expert" doesn't always mean he or she is qualified to provide solid investment advice or that they will be the right fit for you.

Far too many investors have been defrauded by less-than-honest individuals posing as qualified advisors.

You can check out any potential advisor online at the SEC's Investment Advisor Public Disclosure website (*https://adviserinfo.sec.gov/IAPD/Default. aspx*) or BrokerCheck. The North American Securities Administrators Association, another big industry group, also has a very helpful, free online guide that explains the various kinds of financial advisors and suggests important questions to ask when trying to find the right financial advisor for you (*www.nasaa.org/wp-content/uploads/2011/08/Cutting-through-the-Confusion_2013.pdf*).

Additional information is available on state securities regulators' websites (starting at *www.nasaa.org/about-us/contact-us/contact-your-regulator*).

Alphabet Soup

Don't assume, either, that someone is qualified because he or she has alphabet-soup designations after his or her name. Some designations indicate true education and training; others are little more than marketing gimmicks.

FINRA has an online, free data base to help consumers check out and better understand the various financial advisor acronyms, too (*www.finra. org/investors/professional-designations*).

The Next Step

Once your list of potential advisors has been narrowed to only a few, and you've verified their qualifications, you're ready to interview each one.

By now, you're probably thinking, "Enough already. This is too much work just to pick an investment advisor." But this is much more than simply choosing a name. This is your financial future on the line. You're paying for the service; the individual will work for you, so make sure you're thoroughly satisfied with whomever you choose. Talk to each potential candidate before you hand over your money.

Serious About Interviews

When it comes to interviewing prospective advisors, don't be shy about asking questions. Keep asking the questions until you're satisfied with and understand the answers.

This isn't about wasting anyone's time. It's a necessary part of the process. If a potential advisor resents your questions or appears impatient, that's a signal to take your business elsewhere. If he or she doesn't have the time to listen to what you say this early in the process, he or she is even less likely to care what you say or how you think later.

As part of the process, consider asking any potential advisor about his or her background and training as well as the products and services he or she offers, fees and fee structure, and how he or she would communicate with you and manage your account.

Essential Questions

With help from the SEC's Investor.gov website, here are some related questions and explanations to consider when interviewing potential advisors[3]:

- What experience do you have working with people in my same situation and with similar goals? Often the more experience an individual has working with others who share your goals and direction, the better equipped he or she is to suggest the best solutions to fit your needs.

- Do you have experience and training not only in the accumulation phase of investing but also the distribution phase? With your retirement portfolio on the line, the latter is essential.

- What is your education and background, and how does it relate to your work? A potential advisor needn't be an economist, but he or she does need to thoroughly understand the nuances of investing, markets, and the economy.

- What professional licenses and designations do you hold, and what does each one mean? How might they be applicable to my situation? Remember: Alphabet soup doesn't necessarily equate with skill, training, or experience.

- Are you registered with the SEC, a state securities regulator, or FINRA? The SEC cautions investors to make sure any potential advisor is registered to do business in an investor's state.

- Have any disciplinary actions been filed against you with state or federal regulators? If so, what, and how was it resolved? A disciplinary action is not good on someone's record, but the circumstances and how it was resolved matter, too. If a prospective advisor has a disciplinary action on his or her record, give him or her the opportunity to talk about it. If you like the person, the action was resolved satisfactorily, and you're satisfied with the person's explanation, you still may want to consider the individual.

- Have any customer complaints been filed against you? If so, what, and how were they resolved? Again, a complaint isn't advantageous, but it may not be a deal-breaker when you understand the circumstances and how it was resolved. Often we see disgruntled investors simply filing frivolous complaints. Those complaints remain on an advisor's or firm's record, even though there was no deviation from proper procedures or actions.

- Do you offer products specific to your company? If so, how are you compensated and incentivized for selling those products? Some advisors earn more up-front and ongoing if an investor purchases a specific brand product. If it's a good product, that may not be a deal breaker, either, if you know and understand the fees and compensation up-front.

- How are you compensated? How is your company compensated? The key is to be aware of all costs up-front, and make sure ongoing fees and costs are clearly and regularly detailed.

- How are the various fees assessed, and when and how will I be expected to pay them? For example, is a fee due up-front at time of the buy or sale, is it automatically deducted down the road from a portfolio, or is it billed and expected to be paid later?

- Do you offer 24/7 access to an investor's account—online, for example? What kind of security does your website offer? Have there been any breaches of privacy? If so, how were they resolved and what precautions have been taken to prevent further breaches? Easy access to your account information is important.

Potential Services

It's important that any advisor you choose offers the right selection of products and services to meet your needs. Not every advisor offers every product or service.

Also of note, personal financial one-stop shops are growing in popularity. They're organizations that offer or have access to a broad range of personal financial services and specialists in those fields—from brokers to financial, legal, and life-choice advisors. The concept is relationship-building for a lifetime of personal financial services.

If you interview or even hire an investment advisor who is associated with one of those companies, make sure you're not obligated to use only those advisors who the firm designates or is associated with. It's your money, your life, and your choices—not theirs.[4]

When you interview potential advisors, you may want to think about the various services beyond portfolio management that they could provide should you need them. Then you can be sure to ask the right related questions.

Some of those services that you may need in your lifetime include:

- Access to a broad range of securities, including stocks, bonds, ETFs, and mutual funds. For the New ROI purposes, remember that ETFs can be the best option.

- The ability to put together not only your retirement portfolio, but to build a full financial plan to meet your overall needs.

- Access to financial research if you're interested.

- Access to a range of different types of accounts. Do fees change depending on the type of account? Do you offer discounts if clients have multiple types of accounts?

Narrowing the Choices

Once you've narrowed your choice to several potential advisors, the three essentials you must ask to determine your selection are:

1. Who is the most qualified?

2. With whom do I have the best rapport?

3. Who has the best reputation?

Keep in mind that the individual you choose as your financial advisor should be someone who you can count on and trust explicitly—your investing partner. This is not about who wins the popularity contest. The right advisor should meet all the criteria we've discussed. Plus, he or she is the one person who you're comfortable enough with to pick up the phone and turn to for advice, no doubts involved, should you wake up one morning to discover something seriously out of the ordinary—whether economically, politically, personally, or something else.

This is your life, your money, and, with this person's help, your sound financial future on the line.

Last Words

Let's review some of the essentials discussed in this chapter:

- Not everyone is wired for do-it yourself investing success. Not everyone has the discipline for ongoing portfolio monitoring— even if just once a month—or to set the parameters and stick to them day in and day out.

- If you're not a DIY candidate, admit it and find the right advisor to fit your needs.

- Ask friends, family, financial institutions, and experts for the names of recommended advisors.

- Do your homework. Ask the right questions of potential advisors—about background, training, experience, success rates, fees, availability, and much more.

- Not all advisors embrace the New ROI approach to retirement investing.

- Utilize websites like FINRA to learn more about a potential advisor and his or her affiliated company. Be aware, however, that not all complaints automatically should result in dismissing a potential advisor.

- Go back and review all the questions you intend to ask any potential advisor. Be sure to get satisfactory answers to your questions. If someone is impatient with so many questions, move on. If he or she doesn't have time for you before he or she gets your money, chances are there will be even less time for you later.

- It's possible to spend money for advice and still not have the sum devastate your portfolio.

- Make sure you're comfortable with the fees, what services they provide, and how you will be assessed the fees and when.

Now It's Your Turn

To help you take control of your investing portfolio with the New ROI in mind, some questions to ask yourself about your investing, portfolio, and financial future include:

- Are you comfortable with do-it-yourself New ROI retirement investing? If you're not and/or want just a little advice, or a broader approach to your retirement planning, finding the right advisor can be the best approach.

- Do any of your friends or family have an advisor who they like, has done well with their portfolios, and who they would recommend? If so, that recommendation is your first step.

- Does that advisor have any complaints or industry actions (SEC or FINRA, for example) filed against them? If so, thoroughly check out the complaint or action, and then give the individual the opportunity to explain the situation and what happened.

- How much will it cost you in total to hire the individual? That includes fees for investments as well as services. Are you comfortable with that amount?

- Can you access your account anytime? Is it easy? Is your data safe? With the latter, a yes or no answer isn't enough. Find out how your information is protected.

- Are you comfortable with the individual you're considering as an advisor? This is about expertise as well as experience, rapport, personality, accessibility, and more.

11 Making the "New ROI" Work for You, Step by Step

NOW THAT YOU better understand the "New ROI" approach to investing and its primary goal of *reliability of income* in retirement, it's time to determine step-by-step what works best for your money, your portfolio, and your goals.

Start With an Overview

Righting your retirement portfolio begins with a review of the essential elements and related issues of the New ROI process and of your existing portfolio, if applicable.

Remember: It's crucial to take the emotion out of your investment decision-making. Do you have a strategy in place that eliminates emotional decision-making from your portfolio? We all should, no matter the approach each of us takes to investing for retirement.

Let's review step-by-step some of the most important aspects of our process.

Understand the New ROI Mindset

Don't be afraid of or shy away from change. The New ROI is a shift in the traditional approach to retirement investing. Instead of focusing primarily on growing your money, the New ROI emphasizes creating a reliable stream of future income.

That means a strategy that can capitalize on market upsides with built-in protections for your portfolio to ensure that inflation as well as significant losses don't erode your nest egg. With today's volatile markets and highly interconnected marketplaces, the potential for losses is a very real threat to your financial future.

The goal, after all, is to make sure you don't run out of money in your lifetime.

Determine Your Investing Costs

What are the real expenses of your current portfolio holdings? You must consider not only annual fees but ongoing costs when figuring those expenses. Keep in mind that those fees and costs are the easiest changes you can make to your portfolio, and they can have an immediate impact on that portfolio's earnings and growth.

Fees can range across the board and may be assessed for a variety of services and situations, including account maintenance or inactivity. Before you hand over your cash, make sure you know the exact amount of charges, what they are for, when they are assessed, and why. Comparison shop, too. Remember: High fees do *not* equate with big returns.

Conversely, no fees may not be the best approach, either. The key is to be able to justify the fees and still allow your portfolio the ability to achieve significant gains over time. Losses add up—based not only on what's paid out, but also on lost growth as a result of the income paid for fees and services.

Don't be thrown off track by the fine print in contracts with brokers, organizations, or online providers, or in investment prospectuses. Closely reading contracts, prospectuses, and other material is time well-invested, especially in today's heavily hyped investing climate.

If you don't understand a fee or cost, go back to the advisor or the investment organization and insist that they explain it thoroughly until it's clear to you. As an investor, you have the right to customer service and to know how much you're really paying and for what.

Define Your Investing Strategy

Determining the best investing strategy for you, your circumstances, and your needs hinges on understanding your personal risk tolerance. What level of risk to your money are you willing to accept? There is no right or wrong answer to that question.

An acceptable level of investment risk should be one that allows your money to grow while at the same time provides enough protection that you sleep well at night without worrying about your money.

You may want to look again at Chapter 5 and some of the issues discussed that can help you shape your financial future. This is about what makes you feel comfortable and doesn't allow worry about your investments and your financial future to interfere with your life.

Once you understand how much cash you'll need for a comfortable financial future, you can build a portfolio with the right allocations. It's about determining the right amount of equities to produce income for your portfolio, and balancing that with bonds to further ensure capital security, and all within an acceptable level of risk. Equities have the greatest risk and the potential for the greatest return; bonds provide less risk and the potential for less return.

Remember: I like to hold ETFs in each of the economic sectors as well as in bonds because of their relatively lower management costs and broad diversity within a sector or class. That's as opposed to individual stocks or bonds, which offer less diversity and stability.

New ROI returns throughout this book are based on ETF holdings. But the choice of holdings in your portfolio is up to you.

If you decide that you prefer actively managed funds, be sure to do your homework. Do the fund managers have a defined, transparent strategy that's rules-based, that you understand, and that's within your accepted risk tolerance level? What are the real fees and costs associated with an investment? Is the performance worth the cost? Again, don't be afraid to keep asking questions until you are satisfied with the answers.

Aim for True Diversification

Is your portfolio properly diversified? Too often, portfolios don't measure up in terms of spreading out the risk exposure on an investors' money. The mere perception of diversity is not good enough. What's the real risk? That's what matters.

For any retirement portfolio to be truly diversified requires exposure across a broad spectrum of sectors that can react differently to general market ups and downs.

If you already have or are considering index-based investments, learn more about that underlying index. Is it a weighted index? If so, consider the fact that weighting can expose your money to unnecessary risks. Think about what happened to the S&P 500, and holdings that tracked it, when the bottom fell out in 2000 and again in 2008. Those holdings took a terrible financial beating. Can you afford that? Most people can't, especially those nearing or in retirement. Markets are efficient over time. Over long periods of time markets go up. The problem is that very few of us have that long a time line.

You can check out indexes, funds, ETFs, bonds, all kinds of equities, and more online at company Websites as well as industry sites, including:

- **Financial Industry Regulatory Authority (*www.finra.org*).** A nonprofit, nongovernment organization authorized by Congress to protect America's investors by making sure the securities industry operates fairly and honestly; offers information on potential investments, advisors, or brokers as well as information about investing and investments; how to invest; and more.

- **Investor.gov (*https://investor.gov*).** From the U.S. Securities and Exchange Commission, a solid source of research and information on investing, personal finance, and investments; online tools and calculators, as well as government developments related to investing.

- **Morningstar (*www.morningstar.com*).** A world leader in independent investing research; provides listings, performance, ratings, and information on funds, ETFs, stocks, bonds, markets, and more; subscription required for some access.

Minimize Portfolio Losses

Does your portfolio have automatic, built-in stop-loss protections to insulate your money when markets plummet? In today's roller-coaster investing environment, the ups and downs are inevitable, so investors—especially those looking for reliability of income in retirement—need to protect their money.

Losses associated with market downturns can devastate the portfolio of someone nearing or in retirement and on a fixed income. In many cases, portfolios simply can't recover in a reasonable time frame. Yes, markets go up over time—long periods of time. But 20 to 30 years or more is *not* reasonable for someone almost ready to retire or already retired. Even portfolios of younger investors may not be able to recover from major losses and grow to meet financial needs within reasonable time frames.

To reduce the risk of potentially devastating losses requires true maximum diversification—as exemplified by the New ROI equal-sector allocation across a nontraditional 11 sectors.

Discipline in terms of establishing up-front a rules-based portfolio approach and sticking to it also is a necessity to reduce the risk of losses beyond recovery. Setting a stop-loss threshold of a 10-percent drop in the S&P 500 Index—and adhering to it—is essential. No matter what happens, the strategy demands that you remain out of the markets until they recover sufficiently. Sufficient recovery is defined by the New ROI as a 15-percent increase in the S&P 500 from the point at which the index bottoms out— not the point of pullout from the equities market.

In the interim, your money should be temporarily parked in a safe haven like a diversified, conservative bond ETF or U.S. Treasuries.

Find the Right Advisor

Not everyone has or needs a financial advisor to help solidify their retirement goals, assemble the right investment portfolio, monitor it regularly, and make the necessary ongoing adjustments to maintain the right allocations. Some people prefer to do it all themselves. Others like a little or a lot of input from a financial professional. Neither approach is right or wrong. Both can work with the New ROI strategy. It's your personal choice.

If you do take an advisor approach, make sure he or she thoroughly understands and embraces the New ROI. He or she should be focused on transparency and understand the all-important nuances of the retirement or distribution phase of investing. Not all advisors have expertise in that specific realm.

Selecting the right advisor should not depend on how he or she is compensated—whether fee only, a percentage of a portfolio's holdings, a flat rate, or some other fee structure. Rather, choosing an advisor should be based on his or her experience and expertise, as well as the ability to listen and follow through. It helps to like the person, too. The latter, however, should not be the primary or only reason you select a specific advisor.

Don't settle for the first advisor you meet. Research and interview various candidates until you find the best person for the job of working with you to get your future reliability of income in retirement right.

Choosing the Right Investments

One size does *not* fit all when it comes to the makeup of an investment portfolio. The right mix of stocks, bonds, and cash is personal and depends on your age and financial needs. That's yet more reason to ignore the hype about the "latest and greatest" investments online and off that continually bombard us.

The investment ingredients of your retirement portfolio depend on you, your circumstances, and your future needs.

Risk Levels Matter

I hope that by now you better understand investing risk levels and the right moves to make now to ensure a more reliable income stream later. Keep in mind the New ROI approach to portfolio allocation and how it can help you identify the best mix of investment classes to include in your portfolio. That's the optimal allocation of stocks and bonds to meet your needs.

Remember: Stocks offer the most potential for risk/loss and greater potential for return. Within that class, though, the levels of risk or aggressiveness vary dramatically depending on the particular stock, ETF, or mutual fund.

Bonds are at the opposite end of the spectrum: the most conservative, but still with some appreciation. Again, as with stocks, how conservative a bond is varies depending on the quality of the bond or the bond fund. Also, not all bonds are created equal. For purposes of your retirement portfolio, make sure any bonds you choose are investment-grade or U.S. Treasuries.

Cash is available for emergencies or as a temporary place to park your money. It's not a long-term solution; in fact, as we've talked about, when you factor in low interest rates that don't keep pace with inflation, parking your money in cash over the long haul is a money-losing proposition.

Don't assume, either, that once you commit to a specific portfolio mix of stocks and bonds, your allocation formula won't change. In fact, it will and does change depending on your personal circumstances. As you get older, a portfolio normally migrates to more conservative investments to increase capital security.

Solid, Not Speculative, Holdings

Again, the New ROI is designed to capitalize on gains and protect against losses. This approach is not designed to squeeze every dime from every upside of the market.

The holdings in your portfolio should be solid and non-speculative. By now you know I'm a fan of ETFs for their growth potential, diversity, and cost savings. A good barometer is to find a holding that is not actively traded and has low expenses.

Also, make sure that whatever holding you choose is from a well-known company. Bonds should be high-quality or investment-grade only, and from a big company such as BlackRock, Vanguard, State Street, or another company of similar size and rating.

Even in volatile markets, the pricing is likely to be more stable if you stay with larger ETFs. The stock market, after all, is an auction that depends on buyers and sellers. More buyers push prices higher. Conversely, fewer sellers put downward pressure on prices. Some ETFs, for example, have very low trading volume. As a result, when markets become volatile, that means fewer buyers and more sellers, and those ETFs lose some of their stability and liquidity.

Making Your Choices

The choice of investments within your portfolio is up to you. Don't forget, though, that fees and costs add up, and a major tenet of the New ROI is to keep fees low.

If you like the idea of owning stock in individual companies rather than ETFs, which are a market basket of many holdings, you nonetheless could do well to rely on ETFs for the biggest portion of the equities within your portfolio. Then, if you still would like to "play" the markets, you could put aside a small amount of cash as your play money to invest in more speculative or volatile holdings.

Realistically, it's not wise to base the future financial security of you and your loved ones on the volatility of an individual stock. But that shouldn't stop you from still enjoying playing the market on a small scale.

The 11-Sector Approach

After you have determined the right portfolio allocation of stocks and bonds depending on your personal needs, figure out how much money you plan to invest in equities. Then, divide that number by 11, and that's the amount of money in your portfolio that should be invested in each of the 11 sectors. The New ROI relies on equal sector allocation—not weighted sectors—to add a further layer of portfolio protection.

Remember that those 11 sectors are:

- Consumer discretionary.
- Consumer staples.
- Energy.
- Financials.
- Healthcare.
- Industrials.
- Materials.
- Real estate.
- Technology.
- Telecommunications.
- Utilities.

Purchasing Your Investments

To get a thorough overview of what's available as well as better understand the fees and costs associated with any investment, first visit the website linked to a specific investment. Additionally, some companies may allow investors to open an account directly with them. Keep in mind, though, the downside with that approach is that you can be locked into only that company's products; you wouldn't have the option of looking elsewhere for products without going through the process of transferring holdings.

I prefer the freedom of utilizing discount brokers for trading. An independent brokerage allows you to make any trade you wish without pressure one way or the other. We have billions of dollars under management yet we still use discount brokers such as TD Ameritrade for our actual trades because they help save on portfolio fees.

There are a variety of other online discount brokers that you may opt to use. Two notes of caution, however: First, comparison shop. All brokers are not equal in terms of pricing. Second, don't spend your money on free or low-cost advice from those discount brokers.

If you want advice, you may want to consider utilizing a different kind of investment professional—a financial advisor who adheres to the New ROI approach. Whether you want a little advice or a lot, the right advisor can make a big difference for you and your financial future.

Sample Portfolio

Though the choices of investments are up to you, I've put together a sample portfolio with several options (along with their stock symbols) within each of the 11 sectors and across portfolio divisions between stocks, bonds, and cash.

Remember: With the New ROI approach, the equities allocation of your portfolio (depending on your personal risk tolerance level) should be spread equally across 11 different sectors of the economy. That means 9.09 percent of the total equities pie is invested in each of the 11 sectors as represented by an ETF or mutual fund for that specific sector.

Here again are the 11 sectors, along with some suggestions for top-quality ETFs and the expense ratio associated with them:

- Healthcare:
  - ▷ Vanguard Health Care ETF (VHT)/0.09 percent
  - ▷ Health Care Select Sector SPDR Fund (XLV)/0.14 percent
- Consumer discretionary:
  - ▷ Vanguard Consumer Discretionary ETF (VCR)/0.10 percent
  - ▷ Consumer Discretionary Select Sector SPDR Fund (XLY)/0.14 percent
- Consumer staples:
  - ▷ Vanguard Consumer Staples ETF (VDC)/0.10 percent
  - ▷ Consumer Staples Select Sector SPDR Fund (XLP)/0.14 percent
- Technology:
  - ▷ Vanguard Information Technology ETF (VGT)/0.10 percent
  - ▷ Technology Select Sector SPDR Fund (XLK)/0.14 percent
- Financials:
  - ▷ Vanguard Financials ETF (VFH)/0.10 percent
  - ▷ Financial Select Sector SPDR Fund (XLF)/0.14 percent
- Energy:
  - ▷ Vanguard Energy ETF (VDE)/0.10 percent
  - ▷ Energy Select Sector SPDR Fund (XLE)/0.14 percent
- Industrials:
  - ▷ Vanguard Industrials ETF (VIS)/0.10 percent
  - ▷ Industrial Select Sector SPDR Fund (XLI)/0.14 percent
- Telecommunications:
  - ▷ Vanguard Telecommunication Services ETF (VOX)/0.10 percent

- Materials:
  - ▷ Vanguard Materials ETF (VAW)/0.10 percent
  - ▷ Materials Select Sector SPDR Fund (XLB)/0.14 percent
- Utilities:
  - ▷ Vanguard Utilities ETF (VPU)/0.10 percent
  - ▷ Utilities Select Sector SPDR Fund (XLU)/0.14 percent
- Real estate:
  - ▷ Vanguard REIT ETF (VNQ)/0.12 percent

Bond Allocations

In addition to equities holdings, your portfolio also may include some bond allocations. Again, the percentage allocation in your portfolio—if any—depends on your personal needs. Bonds tend to be a more conservative (less risk/less potential for return) than equities.

Whatever your risk level, though, your bond holdings should either be in an investment-grade bond ETF or mutual fund, or U.S. Treasuries.

Following a stop-loss and subsequent equities selloff, with the New ROI strategy, remember that rather than hold your money as cash, it's better to opt temporarily for a high-quality bond ETF or Treasuries. I prefer ETFs. Several solid examples and their expense ratios include:

- Vanguard Total Bond Fund Market Fund (BND)/0.06 percent
- SPDR Bloomberg Barclays Aggregate Bond ETF (BNDS)/0.09 percent
- iShares Core U.S. Aggregate Bond ETF (AGG)/0.06 percent

For investors with a more conservative risk tolerance I prefer bond ETFs that focus on U.S. government bonds:

- Vanguard Intermediate-Term Government Bond ETF (VGIT)/0.10 percent
- SPDR Bloomberg Barclays Intermediate Term Treasury ETF (ITE)/0.10 percent
- iShares 3-7 Year Treasury Bond ETF (IEI)/0.15 percent

Building Your Worksheet

To keep track of your investments and follow the S&P 500 Index more easily, you'll need to build a worksheet. It's probably easiest over the long term to build one on your computer—perhaps an Excel spreadsheet.

But you also can put together one on paper. Just be sure to leave adequate room to track the monthly numbers for the S&P 500 Index and to account for selling and reinvesting your holdings in the event of a stop-loss action.

Follow These Steps

Let's review step by step how to implement your stop-loss plan.

Step 1: Calculate your equity allocation and buy ETFs across all 11 sectors of the economy.

Calculate the right allocation of equities for your objectives, risk tolerance, and age with the help of Chapter 5 and Figure 5.1. Divide your total dollar amount equity allocation by 11, then buy equal amounts of each sector's ETF. For example, if your equity allocation is $250,000 then you will buy $22,727 ($250,000 / 11)—or as close to that dollar amount as possible—of an ETF in each sector.

Step 2: Look up the most recent month-end closing price for the S&P 500 Index (ticker symbol: GSPC).

Write down the most recent month-end closing price for the S&P 500. The most user-friendly website for this is *https://finance.yahoo.com*. Click on the link for the S&P 500. This takes you to a summary page for the S&P 500 (GSPC). Click on the heading "Historical Data." This page provides the closing price for each trading day. Find the most recent month-end price. That's your starting point.

Step 3: Calculate your stop-loss price.

Multiply the most recent month-end closing price for the S&P 500 by 0.90. That number represents the equivalent of a 10-percent drop in the S&P 500. This is your current stop-loss price. For example, if the month-end price for the S&P 500 is 2,100, then your stop-loss price is 1,890 (2,100 x 0.90).

Step 4: Wait one month and again look up the month-end closing price for the S&P 500.

On the first day of each month, look up the S&P 500's closing price for the month that just ended.

Step 5: Determine if you should hold or sell your equities.

If the latest month-end price is greater than the stop-loss price, then hold your equity investments and move to Step 6.

If the current month-end price of the S&P 500 is less than the stop-loss price, then sell your equity investments and move to Step 7.

Step 6: Update your current stop-loss price.

Multiply the most recent month-end closing price for the S&P 500 by 0.90 just as in Step 2. For example, if the month-end price for the S&P 500 is 1,950, then your stop-loss price is 1,755 (1,950 x 0.90). Compare this value to your current stop-loss price. The higher of these two numbers becomes your current stop-loss price. For example, if your current stop-loss price is 1,890 and the new stop-loss price is 1,755, then you continue to use your current stop-loss price of 1,890. However, if your current stop-loss price is less than the new stop-loss price of 1,755, then you will use 1,755 as your stop-loss price next month.

Continue to repeat steps 4, 5, and 6 on the first day of each month until the numbers signal that you must sell your equities. Once you sell your equities, then you are ready for Step 7.

Step 7: Buy a high-quality bond ETF.

Take the proceeds you receive from the sale of your equity positions and buy a high-quality bond ETF.

Step 8: Calculate your buy-back price.

Multiply the most recent month-end closing price for the S&P 500 by 1.15. That number represents a 15-percent increase in the S&P 500 from its low point. This is your current buy-back price. For example, if the month-end price for the S&P 500 is 1,600, then your buy-back price is 1,840 (1,600 x 1.15).

Step 9: Wait one month and look up the month-end closing price for the S&P 500.

On the first day of each month, look up the most recent month-end closing price for the S&P 500.

Step 10: Determine if you should hold or sell your bond position.

If that new month-end price is less than the buy-back price, then hold your bond investment and move to Step 11.

If that month-end price is greater than the buy-back price, then sell your bond investment and return to Step 1.

Step 11: Update your current stop-loss price.

Multiply the most recent month-end closing price for the S&P 500 by 1.15 just as you did in Step 8. For example, if the month-end price for the S&P 500 is 1,500, then your buy-back price is 1,725 (1,500 x 1.15). Compare this value to your current buy-back price. The lowest of these two values becomes your current buy-back price. For example, if your current buy-back price is 1,840 and the new buy-back price is 1,725, then you continue to use your current buy-back price of 1,725. However, if your current buy-back price is greater than the new stop-loss price of 1,725, then you will use 1,725 as your buy-back price next month.

Continue to repeat steps 9, 10, and 11 on the first day of each month until the numbers indicate it's time to sell your bond position. Once you sell your bond position, then you're ready for Step 1 again.

More Details to Remember

Remember to always check the S&P 500 Index and your portfolio holdings' numbers at the close of business on the last day of each month. You can check either Yahoo/Finance, Google/Finance, or a preferred search engine or website. Regardless of how or where you gather your data, be sure to write down the numbers. That makes it easier to keep tabs on the numbers month-to-month.

Once a month is frequent enough to check the S&P numbers, but if you prefer to check the markets more often, that's okay, too. It's your preference—as long as you pay attention to the New ROI's pre-determined parameters. This isn't a portfolio churn approach to retirement investing. It's about growing your money to ensure long-term reliable returns.

After a sell-off and the index increases 15 percent from the point at which it bottomed out, it's time to reinvest your initial capital plus the gains equally across those 11 sector equities. The easiest way to do that is to re-purchase the same ETFs or holdings that you sold.

It's that simple. Don't fret a 14-percent increase. This isn't about greed; it's about preserving and holding on to gains with the goal of reliability of income in retirement. A 14-percent gain is not the right time to return to equities. Our research has shown that until a market increases 15 percent, it may not be done with its seesaw recovery.

And, you can sleep soundly knowing that, no matter how the market drops, you've minimized your losses to a level that is manageable and recoverable.

Tips and Cautions

Once your New ROI portfolio is in place, don't be swayed to change the New ROI pre-set rules of when, what, and how to buy; or when and how to sell; and what to do with the cash. All the hype, hot tickets, "insightful" research, and lots more of the noise are not the way to create reliability of income in retirement. It's your financial future on the line. Bet on a reliable choice—not a hot one.

If after several months or years, you're no longer comfortable with your portfolio's allocation between stocks and bonds, you can change it. But keep in mind the numbers we talked about in Chapter 5, and make sure that however you adjust your allocations, you'll still have the growth potential you need to meet your income withdrawal needs in retirement.

Whatever the split in your portfolio among stocks and bonds, though, always make sure the portfolio is invested in high-quality bond funds and/ or high-quality sector funds. After all, the New ROI should be about peace of mind, both now and later.

Last Words

Let's review some of the essentials discussed in this chapter:

- Begin your New ROI approach to retirement investing by first thoroughly understanding all tenets of investing for reliability of retirement income in mind, how to do it, and why.

- With or without the help of an advisor, the New ROI is about positioning your money to capitalize on the growth potential offered by market upswings, while protecting it from extreme losses on the downside.

- Aim for true diversification in your portfolio with the help of an equal allocation across 11 sectors of the economy.

- Do your homework when it comes to fees and costs associated with investments and advisors. It's not about buying what sounds the least expensive; it's about knowing all the fees involved in an investment.

- Set up and use a worksheet—either on a computer or a pad of paper—to keep track of your investments, your moves, and the monthly closings for the S&P 500 Index.

- Once a month at the same time every month, check the S&P 500 Index. If it's down 10 percent from the high since you bought, it's time to sell.

- Move the cash into a temporary safe haven until the S&P 500 is up 15 percent from its bottoming out. Then it's time to buy back all 11-sector equities holdings.

- Discipline matters. Stick to the process, the pre-set rules, and the simple procedures and your portfolio will have the chance to grow and build for a sound financial future into and throughout your retirement.

Now It's Your Turn

To help you take control of your investing portfolio with the New ROI in mind, some questions to ask yourself about your investing, portfolio, and financial future include:

- Are you willing to take control of your retirement investing future with the help of the New ROI approach? In these pages, I've shared with you step-by-step how to get it done.

- Are you up to DIY retirement investing? If you're not and don't honestly think you will be able to adhere to and follow through on the New ROI rules-based approach no matter what, then find the right financial advisor to help you.

- Are you honest with yourself in terms of how much risk you're willing tolerate with your retirement investments? That's an essential part of peace of mind investing.

- If you really enjoy the challenge of playing/gambling on the market, have you set aside a small amount of money to do so? Your retirement portfolio is not the vehicle for that. Your future reliability of income in retirement is at stake.

- Are your ready to get started on righting your retirement portfolio? If so, then let's do it now.

Glossary

401(k) fees. The cost of operating and administering a 401(k) plan; in addition to annual operating expense of a mutual fund, for example; passed on to plan participants.

Alpha. Risk-adjusted measure of an investment's performance against a benchmark.

Annual operating expenses. ETFs and mutual funds are managed by investment professionals who incur costs for their services that are passed on to investors as fees deducted from the fund's assets; can include management fees, 12b-1 fees, and other expenses; often referred to as a percentage of the fund's assets—the fund's expense ratio (identified in the fund's prospectus as the total annual fund operating expenses).

Asset-weighted index. A stock index based on or weighted by the underlying market value of its holdings; also known as a capitalization-weighted index. The S&P 500 Index, for example, is an asset or capitalization-weighted index. That means the percentage of a company's holdings in the S&P 500 Index at any time depend on a company's market value or size. Bigger companies with larger market value make up a larger portion of the index compared with smaller companies with lower market value.

Back-testing. The use of historical market data or simulations to analyze future performance of an investment or investing strategy.

Basis point. A measurement of the percent change in value of a financial instrument; 1 basis point equal 0.01 percent.

Beta. A measure of a stock's volatility in relation to the rest of the market; the S&P 500 Index with a beta of 1.00 is the benchmark; a stock with a beta of greater than 1.00 is considered more volatile than the market in general as measured by the benchmark, whereas a stock with a beta of less than 1.0 is less volatile; also known as beta coefficient.

Black box strategy. Investing strategy that relies on gut or intuition as opposed to fact; the downside is an investor doesn't know what's inside the box—what to expect or do with his or her investments in response to an external event.

Commission. Compensation a firm or financial professional can earn acting as an agent in your securities transaction; even low-cost, discount brokerages earn some fee for their services.

Diversifiable risk. A form of risk that tends to be company- or sector-related; a problem with a particular product or a labor dispute, for example, that can affect a holding price; can be minimized with portfolio diversification; also known as unsystematic risk.

Expense ratio. A mutual fund's total annual expenses expressed as a percentage of its net assets; a 1-percent expense ratio translates to $10 for every $1,000 invested, whereas a $10,000 investment with a 1-percent expense ratio carries a $100 annual expense.

Growth companies. Successful companies that are expanding and experiencing above average growth with strong underlying fundamentals.

Investment advisory fees. Can be charged by a professional investment advisor to manage your portfolio; annual and can be fixed or based on a percentage of portfolio's value.

Large capitalization companies. Big companies with market capitalization (value of its outstanding shares) generally of more than $5 billion; also known as large-cap companies.

Markdown. When a security is sold to an investor at a price lower than market price, the difference or discount is the markdown.

Market capitalization. The value of a company's outstanding shares.

Market value. The number of outstanding shares in a company multiplied by the share price.

Markup. A broker/dealer who sells you a security from its inventory is a principal in the transaction and is compensated for that by selling the security to you at higher than market price—the markup.

Ongoing fee. Regular expenses incurred by an investment like a mutual fund or ETF; could include annual maintenance or management expenses.

Risk tolerance. The level of risk that an investor is willing to accept when it comes to his or her investments.

Sales load. A mutual fund can charge a fee similar to a commission; can be front-end, assessed at the time of purchase, or back-end, at time of sale.

Small capitalization companies. Smaller companies generally with market capitalization of $300 million to $2 billion, though the numbers can vary; also known as small-cap companies.

Standard deviation. In investing, a number that uses an investment's annual rate of return as an indicator of its volatility; measuring how much (if at all) and in what direction (up or down) that investment historically moves from its mean (average); the greater the number, the more volatile the investment.

Surrender charge. Typically, assessed for early withdrawal, from an annuity, for example; often a percentage of amount withdrawn.

Systematic risk. The entire market is exposed to this form of risk from external forces like interest rates, recession, and wars. Holdings diversification doesn't necessarily protect a portfolio from these risks; also known as undiversifiable risk.

Transaction fee. Cost incurred when you buy, sell, or trade an investment.

Undiversifiable risk. See *Systematic risk*.

Value company. A company whose stock generally trades at a lower price relative to its fundamentals; potentially considered undervalued.

Notes

Chapter 1

1. National Center for Health Statistics, "United States, 2015: With Special Feature on Racial and Ethnic Health Disparities," Hyattsville, Md., p. 21, *www.cdc.gov/nchs/data/hus/hus15.pdf#014%20.*

2. "Life Expectancy for Social Security," Social Security Administration Website, *www.ssa.gov/history/lifeexpect.html.*

3. "Running Out of Money Is Top Retirement Concern, Says AICPA Survey of Financial Planners," American Institute of CPAs press release, October 6, 2016, *www.aicpa.org/Press/PressReleases/2016/Pages/Running-Out-of-Money-Top-Retirement-Concern-Financial-Planners.aspx.* Accessed October 12, 2016.

4. Employee Benefit Research Institute, Notes, "Amount of Savings Needed for Health Expenses for People Eligible for Medicare," *Vol. 36, No. 10* (October 2015), *www.ebri.org/pdf/notespdf/EBRI_Notes_10_Oct15_HlthSvgs_DB-DC.pdf.*

5. S&P Dow Jones Indices, "S&P 500 2015: Global Sales, *https://us.spindices.com/search/?query=S%26P+500+2014+global+sales&Search=GO&sortType=Relevance&resultsPerPage=25.*

6. Poterba, James M. "Retirement Security in an Aging Society," *American Economic Review 104* (May 2014): 1–33.

Chapter 2

1. U.S. Government Accountability Office, "Financial Regulatory Reform: Financial Crisis Losses and Potential Impacts of the Dodd-Frank Act," January 2013, *www.gao.gov/assets/660/651322.pdf.*

Chapter 3

1. Taylor, Jay, "Is a Biotech Bubble Looming," Wyatt Investment Research, April 14, 2015, *www.wyattresearch.com/article/biotech-bubble.*

2. Yellen, Janet, speech to "Finance and Society," a conference sponsored by Institute for New Economic Thinking, Washington, D.C., May 6, 2015, *www.federalreserve.gov/newsevents/speech/yellen20150506a.htm.*

3. *www.gurufocus.com.*

4. CRSP Survivor-Bias-Free Mutual Fund Database (CRSP® Data), provided courtesy of the University of Chicago on behalf of its Center for Research in Security Prices at Chicago Booth and Standard & Poor's Index Services Group, *www.crsp.com/products/crsp-historical-indexes.* CRSP and its third-party suppliers use best efforts to obtain information appearing on its CRSP Data from sources and methods considered reliable. The CRSP Data is provided "as is." In no event shall the University of Chicago, the Booth School of Business, CRSP and/or its third-party suppliers be liable for the accuracy of the CRSP Data, or for decisions made or actions taken based on this CRSP Data.

5. S&P Dow Jones Indices, "SPIVA® U.S. Scorecard," *https://us.spindices.com/documents/spiva/spiva-us-yearend-2015.pdf.*

6. "SEC Charges Investment Manager F-Squared and Former CEO With Making False Performance Claims: F-Squared Settles Case by Paying $35 Million and Admitting Wrongdoing," Securities and Exchange Commission press release, December 22, 2014, *www.sec.gov/news/ pressrelease/2014-289.html*. Accessed September 12, 2016.

7. "Investment Advisers Paying Penalties for Advertising False Performance Claims," Securities and Exchange Commission press release, Aug. 25, 2016, *www.sec.gov/news/ pressrelease/2016-167.html*. Accessed September 12, 2016.

Chapter 4

1. "Dalbar Pinpoints Investor Pain," Dalbar Inc. press release, *www.dalbar.com/Portals/dalbar/cache/News/PressReleases/ DALBAR%20Pinpoints%20Investor%20Pain%202015.pdf*. Accessed May 15, 2016.

2. "Better Investment Recommendations Equals Greater Returns?" Dalbar Inc. press release, April 26, 2016, *www. dalbar.com/Portals/dalbar/cache/News/PressReleases/QAIB%20 2016%20Press%20Release%20v1.pdf*. Accessed May 15, 2016.

3. Dalbar Inc. website, *www.dalbar.com*.

4. Gibson, Thomas. *The Facts About Speculation*. Cosimo Classics.

5. Hale, Nathan, CBS Moneywatch, "Lessons From a Great Fund Manager's Record," July 16, 2010, *www.cbsnews.com/news/ lessons-from-a-great-fund-managers-record*.

6. *www.apmex.com/spotprices/gold-price*.

Chapter 6

1. U.S. Government Accountability Office, "Financial Regulatory Reform: Financial Crisis Losses and Potential Impacts of the Dodd-Frank Act," January 2013, *www.gao.gov/assets/660/651322.pdf*.

2. AARP Public Policy Institute, "The Impact of the Financial Crisis on Older Americans," p. 6, *http://assets.aarp.org/rgcenter/econ/i19_crisis.pdf; www.beaconinvesting.com/adviser-toolbox/BEA_White_Paper_Stop_Loss*.

3. Israelsen, Craig L., "The Benefits of Low Correlation," *www.7twelveportfolio.com/Downloads/Benefits-of-Low-Correlation-JourOfIndexes-200711.pdf*.

Chapter 8

1. General Motors 10-K for period ended December 31, 2015, filed with Securities and Exchange Commission, *www.gm.com/content/dam/gm/en_us/english/Group4/InvestorsPDFDocuments/10-K.pdf*.

2. "Facts on Microsoft," *www.statista.com/topics/823/microsoft*.

3. "Starbucks Strengthens Commitment in China," Starbucks press release, January 12, 2016, press release, *https://news.starbucks.com/news/starbucks-strengthens-commitment-in-china-2016*. Accessed December 13, 2016.

4. S&P Dow Jones Indices, McGraw-Hill Financial, "The New GICS Real Estate Sector and S&P U.S. Benchmarks," *www.spindices.com/documents/additional-material/spdji-the-new-gics-real-estate-sector-and-sp-us-benchmarks.pdf*.

5. "Deepwater Horizon: BP Gulf of Mexico Oil Spill," U.S. Environmental Protection Agency Website, *www.epa.gov/enforcement/deepwater-horizon-bp-gulf-mexico-oil-spill*.

Chapter 9

1. "Investor Research Report," Siegal & Gale LLC, July 26, 2012, *www.sec.gov/news/studies/2012/917-financial-literacy-study-part3.pdf*, p. 171.

2. Laurent Barras, Oliver Scaillet, and Russ Wermers, "False Discoveries in Mutual Fund Performance: Measuring Luck in Estimated Alphas," *The Journal of Finance, LXV, No. 1* (February 2010), *http://alex2.umd.edu/wermers/FDR_published.pdf*.

3. "Infographic: The Keys to Active Management Success," Vanguard website, *https://advisors.vanguard.com/VGApp/iip/site/advisor/researchcommentary/article/IWE_InvResKeysActiveMgtInfograph*.

4. Todorova, Aleksandra, "Are You Guilty of Making These Investing Mistakes," SigFig website, May 7, 2015, *https://blog.sigfig.com/index.php/investing-advice/are-you-guilty-of-making-these-investing-mistakes/?utm_source=marketingpages&utm_medium=web&utm_campaign=footer*.

5. Ibid.

6. "Average Cost of Online Trading," ValuePenguin website, *www.valuepenguin.com/average-cost-online-brokerage-trading*.

7. "Average Expense Ratios for Equity, Hybrid, and Bond Mutual Funds Hit 20-Year Lows," Investment Company Institute press release, March 16, 2016, *www.ici.org/pressroom/news/16_news_trends_expenses*. Accessed October 12, 2016.

8. Ibid.

9. "2015 Fee Study: Investors Are Driving Expense Ratios Down," Morningstar press release, *https://news.morningstar.com/pdfs/2015_fee_study.pdf*. Accessed December 9, 2016.

Chapter 10

1. "Better Investment Recommendations Equals Greater Returns? Quantitative Analysis of Investor Behavior 2016," Dalbar Inc. press release, April 26, 2016, *www.dalbar.com/ Portals/dalbar/cache/News/PressReleases/QAIB%202016%20 Press%20Release%20v1.pdf.* Accessed May 15, 2016.

2. "IRAs—Distributions (Withdrawals)," International Revenue Service website, *www.irs.gov/retirement-plans/ retirement-plans-faqs-regarding-iras-distributions-withdrawals.*

3. "Investor Bulletin: Top Tips for Selecting a Financial Professional," *https://investor.gov/ additional-resources/news-alerts/alerts-bulletins/ investor-bulletin-top-tips-selecting-financial.*

4. Ibid.

Index

About the Author

CHRIS COOK, entrepreneur and investment manager, is a strong proponent of improving investing outcomes with the application of scientific fundamentals. He's founder and president of Dayton, Ohio–based Beacon Capital Management, a leading consultant to and award-winning asset manager for financial advisors and institutional investors in developing globally diversified portfolios to optimize long-term performance. He's also the go-to source for a variety of media outlets on investment and financial topics for both consumer and industry audiences.

His firm, Beacon Capital Management, has been recognized as one of the most innovative investment advisory firms in the industry by Wealth & Finance International, and it directly manages more than $2 billion in assets. Beacon also was honored by *Financial Times* as a Top Registered Investment Advisor of 2016 and was named as one of the Top 100 RIA Firms of 2016 by RIA Channel.

Cook holds a variety of licenses from FINRA (Financial Industry Regulatory Authority), including Series 7 (General Securities Representative Qualification Examination), Series 4 (Registered Options Principal Examination), Series 24 (General Securities Principal Qualifications, applicable to supervisory management of a general securities broker-dealer), and Series 53 (Municipal Securities Principal Qualification Examination); and from NASAA (North American Securities Administrators Association),

Series 63 (Uniform Securities State Law Examination) and Series 65 (Investment Advisers Law Examination).

He is a graduate of Bowling Green State University with a bachelor of science in business administration and a concentration in finance.